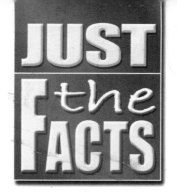

WORLD ATLAS

This edition published in the United States in 2006 by School Specialty Publishing, a member of the School Specialty Family. Copyright © ticktock Entertainment Ltd 2005 First published in Great Britain in 2005 by ticktock Media Ltd. Printed in China.

Written by Dee Phillips. Special thanks to: Alan Grimwade, Cosmographics, Indexing Specialists (UK) Ltd, and Elizabeth Wiggans.

Library of Congress-in-Publication Data is on file with the publisher.

Send all inquiries to:
School Specialty Publishing
8720 Orion Place
Columbus, OH 43240-2111

ISBN 0-7696-4260-8
1 2 3 4 5 6 7 8 9 10 TTM 11 10 09 08 07 06

CONTENTS

HOW TO USE THIS BOOK

JUST THE FACTS, WORLD ATLAS combines detailed world maps with a quick and easy-to-use way to research geography facts and find information on the world's people, cities, countries, rivers, lakes, and mountains. Each of the world's continents has its own section. In addition, there are pages containing facts about the solar system, time zones, landforms, earthquakes, volcanoes, and the oceans. For fast access to just the facts, follow the tips on these pages.

BOX HEADINGS
Look for heading words linked to your research to guide you to the right fact box.

CONTINENT-BY-CONTINENT FACTS
Each continent's section opens with two pages that show key facts and statistics about the people and geography of that continent.

TWO QUICK WAYS TO FIND A FACT:

1 Use the detailed **CONTENTS** list on page 3 to find your topic of interest.

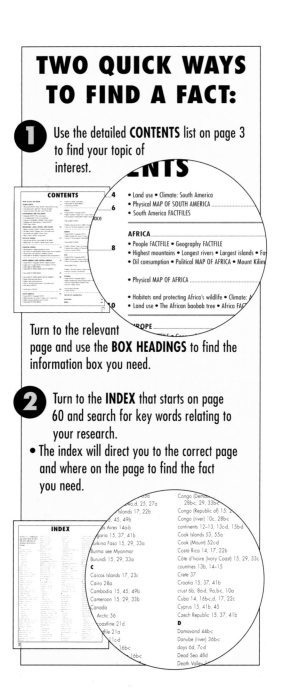

Turn to the relevant page and use the **BOX HEADINGS** to find the information box you need.

2 Turn to the **INDEX** that starts on page 60 and search for key words relating to your research.
• The index will direct you to the correct page and where on the page to find the fact you need.

• See page 33
AFRICA FACTFILES

PEOPLE FACTFILE

Total population:
887,000,000

Highest population:
Nigeria 128,771,988

Lowest population:
Djibouti 476,703

Most populous city:
Cairo, Egypt
11,146,000 residents

Life expectancy:
Male: 51 years
Female: 53 years

Highest infant mortality rate:
Angola: 191 deaths per 1,000 births – the highest in the world

• See the GLOSSARY for definitions of LIFE EXPECTANCY and INFANT MORTALITY RATE.

Average annual income per person (in USD):
Highest: Mauritius $12,800
Lowest: Sierra Leone $600

GEOGRAPHY FACTFILE

Total land area:
11,697,000 square miles

Largest country:
Sudan: 967,499 square miles

Smallest country:
Mayotte: 144 square miles

Largest lake:
Lake Victoria, East Africa
26,641 square miles

Largest desert:
Sahara Desert, North Africa
3.5 million square miles
Largest desert in the world

Highest waterfall:
Tugela Falls, South Africa
Total drop: 3,110 feet

• See page 33
AFRICA FACTFILES

28

AFRICA

Africa is the second largest continent in the world. The world's biggest desert, the Sahara, dominates the landscape of the north, while in the south forests and vast grasslands are home to wild animals, such as leopards, lions, and elephants. The Great Rift Valley, one of the Earth's major geological features, runs from the Red Sea down to Mozambique. This huge crack in the Earth's surface, caused by a series of faults, is made up of mountains, volcanoes, deep valleys, and lakes.

An African leopard in the Samburu Game Reserve, Kenya.

HIGHEST MOUNTAINS

NAME	LOCATION	HEIGHT (feet)
Mt. Kilimanjaro	Tanzania	19,341
Mt. Kirinyaga (Mt. Kenya)	Kenya	17,060
Mount Stanley (Margherita Peak)	Dem. Rep. Congo/Uganda	16,765
Ras Dashen	Ethiopia	15,157

LONGEST RIVERS

NAME	RIVER MOUTH	LENGTH (miles)
Nile	Mediterranean	4,144
Congo	Atlantic Ocean	2,900
Niger	Atlantic Ocean	2,597
Zambezi	Indian Ocean	2,200

LARGEST ISLANDS

NAME		AREA (sq miles)
Madagascar	Indian Ocean	226,657
Réunion	Indian Ocean	972

• See page 11 WORLD'S 10 LARGEST LAKES

OIL CONSUMPTION

The amount of oil produced, bought and sold, and used in the world is measured in barrels. A barrel is equivalent to 42 gallons.

Nigeria is Africa's largest producer of oil — 2,356,000 barrels per day

TOP 5 CONSUMERS OF OIL (USAGE PER DAY)	
Egypt	562,000 barrels
South Africa	460,000 barrels
Nigeria	275,000 barrels
Libya	216,000 barrels
Algeria	209,000 barrels

FAST FACTS

• Almost 90% of the rainforest in West Africa has been destroyed.

• 90% of the rainforest on the African island of Madagascar has been destroyed. Around 80% of the animal species found on Madagascar live only on this island and nowhere else on Earth (other than zoo populations).

• See page 24 AMAZON RAINFOREST FACTS

• Namibia was the first country in the world to include protecting the environment in its constitution. Around 14% of Namibia is now protected including the entire Namib Desert coast.

• Ancient rock paintings show that 8,000 years ago the Sahara Desert was a lush, green place that was home to many wild animals.

• It is believed that the first place in the world to cultivate coffee was Ethiopia. It was grown in the Kefa region of Ethiopia around 1000 years ago.

LINKS
Look for the purple links throughout the book. Each link gives other pages where related or additional facts can be found.

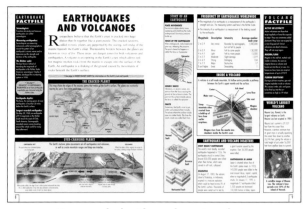

Pages packed with supplementary facts
and geography information.

FACTFILES The section for each continent includes a file of
information on every country.

POLITICAL MAPS
Each continent has a map that shows the
territories of all the countries.

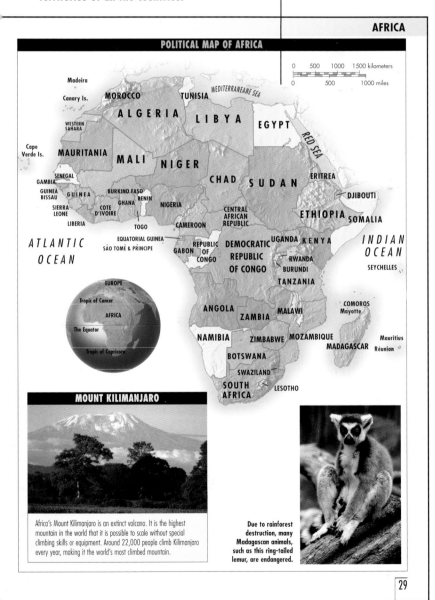

POLITICAL MAP OF AFRICA

AFRICA

| 0 | 500 | 1000 | 1500 kilometers |
| 0 | 500 | | 1000 miles |

Madeira

Canary Is.

MOROCCO   TUNISIA   MEDITERRANEANE SEA

WESTERN
SAHARA   ALGERIA   LIBYA   EGYPT

RED SEA

Cape
Verde Is.   MAURITANIA   MALI   NIGER   CHAD   SUDAN   ERITREA

SENEGAL   DJIBOUTI
GAMBIA   BURKINO FASO   NIGERIA   CENTRAL
GUINEA   BENIN   AFRICAN   ETHIOPIA   SOMALIA
BISSAU   GUINEA   GHANA   REPUBLIC
SIERRA   COTE   TOGO
LEONE   D'IVOIRE   CAMEROON

LIBERIA   EQUATORIAL GUINEA   UGANDA   KENYA   INDIAN
SÃO TOMÉ & PRINCIPE   REPUBLIC   DEMOCRATIC   OCEAN
ATLANTIC   GABON   OF   REPUBLIC
OCEAN   CONGO   OF CONGO   RWANDA
BURUNDI   SEYCHELLES
TANZANIA

EUROPE
Tropic of Cancer   COMOROS
ANGOLA   Mayotte
AFRICA   ZAMBIA   MALAWI
The Equator
NAMIBIA   ZIMBABWE   MOZAMBIQUE   Mauritius
Tropic of Capricorn   MADAGASCAR   Réunion
BOTSWANA
SWAZILAND
SOUTH   LESOTHO
AFRICA

MOUNT KILIMANJARO

Africa's Mount Kilimanjaro is an extinct volcano. It is the highest
mountain in the world that it is possible to scale without special
climbing skills or equipment. Around 22,000 people climb Kilimanjaro
every year, making it the world's most climbed mountain.

Due to rainforest
destruction, many
Madagascan animals,
such as this ring-tailed
lemur, are endangered.

29

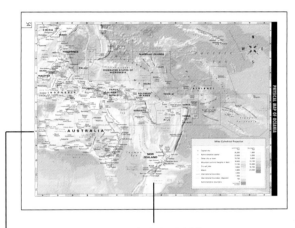

PHYSICAL MAPS
Each continent has a detailed physical
map that shows:
- Borders
- Capital cities
- Major cities
- Highest mountains
- Rivers and lakes
- Land heights above and below sea level
- Oceans, seas, and major bodies of water

HOW TO FIND A PLACE USING
THE PHYSICAL MAPS
Look up the place you want to find in the MAP INDEX
on page 60–64. There you will see a page number
and a letter/number code. Look for the letter and
number on the grid at the edge of the relevant page.
Draw a line with your fingers from those two points.
You will find the place you are looking for where the
two tracks meet.

GLOSSARY
A GLOSSARY of words and terms used in this book
begins on page 58.

The glossary provides additional information
to supplement the facts on the main pages.

JUST THE FACTS
Each topic box presents the facts you need
in lists; short, quick-to-read bullet points;
charts, and tables

Age of the Earth:
4.5 billion years old

Diameter at the Equator:
7,926 miles across

Diameter at the Poles:
7,900 miles across

Circumference at the Equator:
23,627 miles around

Weight (mass) of the Earth:
6.6 sextillion tons

Average surface temperature:
59°F

Rotational speed at the Equator:
995 mph
The Earth is a ball spinning on an axis, so places at the Equator spin much faster than at the North and South Poles.

M O O N
FACTFILE

A moon is a ball of rock that orbits a planet. Moons are sometimes called satellites. The Earth has one moon.

Length of Moon's orbit:
The Moon orbits the Earth once every 27 days, 7 hours, and 43 minutes. It takes the same length of time to rotate once on its own axis.

Orbiting speed:
2300 mph

Distance from the Earth:
The distance varies from 221,456–238,857 miles.

Circumference of the Moon:
6,790 miles around the middle

PLANET EARTH

Our planet, called *Earth*, is a ball of rock traveling about 67,000 miles an hour through space. Earth is moving around a star, called the *Sun*. The pulling power, or gravity, of the Sun keeps the Earth on an elliptical (oval-shaped) course. The time it takes the Earth to make one complete orbit of the Sun is called a *year*.

The Earth is one of nine planets that make up the Solar System.

PLANET EARTH FROM SPACE

When viewed from space the Earth looks blue, brown and white.

The vast areas of blue are oceans. 70.7% of the Earth's surface is covered in water: an area of 138,984,000 square miles.

The brown areas are landmasses. 29.3% of the Earth's surface is dry land: an area of 57,688,000 square miles.

The white areas are clouds hanging in the atmosphere (the layer of gases surrounding the Earth).

INSIDE PLANET EARTH

The crust
Thickness varies from 3 miles (beneath the oceans) to 12–43 miles (where there are landmasses and mountains).

The mantle
Made of magnesium and silicon and around 1,800 miles thick. About 62 miles down, the mantle becomes molten (melted).

Outer core
Made of molten iron, cobalt, and nickel and around 1,400 miles thick.

Inner core
Made of solid iron and around 800 miles thick. The temperature at the core is 10,800°F.

EARTH TIME

A year
The exact time it takes for the Earth to make one complete orbit of the Sun is 365 days, 6 hours, 9 minutes and 10 seconds.

A leap year
Because it is more convenient to use a calendar of 365 whole days, every four years we have to add up the extra 6 hours, 9 minutes and 10 seconds to make an extra day. These 366-day years are called leap years.

A day
As the Earth orbits the Sun it also rotates, or spins around. One complete rotation takes 23 hours, 56 minutes and 4 seconds. We round this period up to 24 hours and call it a day.

HOT AND COLD PLANET

Because the Earth is curved like a ball, the Sun's rays are weaker and more spread out at the Arctic and Antarctic, making these regions cold.

At the Equator, the Sun's rays are the most concentrated, so this region is very hot.

Earth is dividied into different sections by human beings sothat it is easier to study.

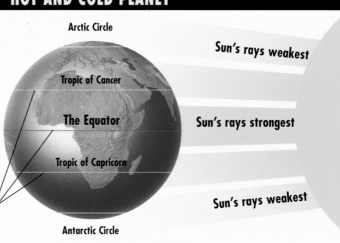

Arctic Circle

Tropic of Cancer

The Equator

Tropic of Capricorn

Antarctic Circle

Sun's rays weakest

Sun's rays strongest

Sun's rays weakest

SUMMER AND WINTER

As Earth spins, it also tilts, so its position in relation to the Sun gradually changes throughout the year.

When the northern hemisphere is tilted toward the Sun, countries in the north have summer. Countries in the southern hemisphere have winter.

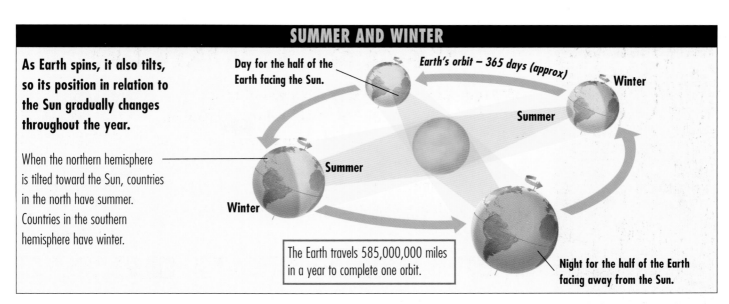

Day for the half of the Earth facing the Sun.

Earth's orbit – 365 days (approx)

Winter

Summer

Summer

Winter

The Earth travels 585,000,000 miles in a year to complete one orbit.

Night for the half of the Earth facing away from the Sun.

THE SOLAR SYSTEM

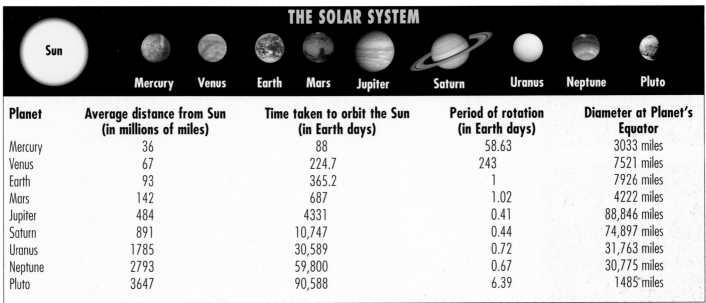

Sun — Mercury — Venus — Earth — Mars — Jupiter — Saturn — Uranus — Neptune — Pluto

Planet	Average distance from Sun (in millions of miles)	Time taken to orbit the Sun (in Earth days)	Period of rotation (in Earth days)	Diameter at Planet's Equator
Mercury	36	88	58.63	3033 miles
Venus	67	224.7	243	7521 miles
Earth	93	365.2	1	7926 miles
Mars	142	687	1.02	4222 miles
Jupiter	484	4331	0.41	88,846 miles
Saturn	891	10,747	0.44	74,897 miles
Uranus	1785	30,589	0.72	31,763 miles
Neptune	2793	59,800	0.67	30,775 miles
Pluto	3647	90,588	6.39	1485 miles

TIME ZONES

As the Earth spins, some parts of the world are in sunlight while others are in darkness. That is why it is a different time in various places in the world.

Therefore, the world has been divided up into 24 time zones. Because the Earth rotates through 360 degrees every 24 hours, each time zone covers 15 degrees of longitude on a map of the world.

The zero point of longitude is at Greenwich in London. It is known as the *Greenwich meridian*. As you move east or west from Greenwich through each new time zone, you add or subtract an hour of time.

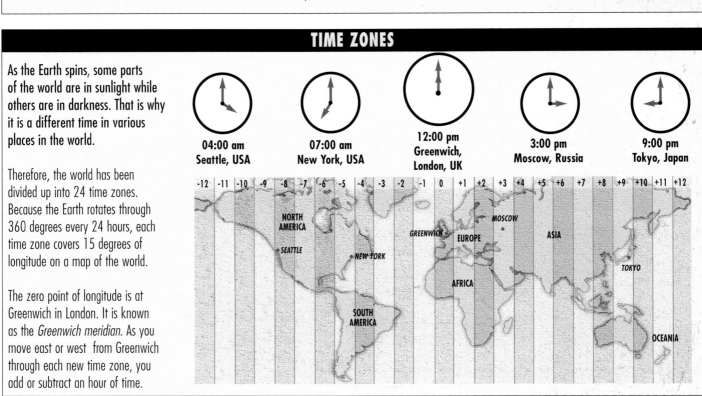

04:00 am
Seattle, USA

07:00 am
New York, USA

12:00 pm
Greenwich,
London, UK

3:00 pm
Moscow, Russia

9:00 pm
Tokyo, Japan

-12 -11 -10 -9 -8 -7 -6 -5 -4 -3 -2 -1 0 +1 +2 +3 +4 +5 +6 +7 +8 +9 +10 +11 +12

NORTH AMERICA · SEATTLE · NEW YORK · GREENWICH · EUROPE · MOSCOW · ASIA · AFRICA · SOUTH AMERICA · TOKYO · OCEANIA

EARTHQUAKES AND VOLCANOES

Researchers believe that the Earth's crust is cracked into huge pieces that fit together like a giant puzzle. The cracked sections, called *tectonic plates*, are supported by the oozing, soft rocks of the mantle beneath the Earth's crust. The unstable borders between the plates are known as *rings of fire*. These areas are danger zones for both volcanoes and earthquakes. A volcano is an opening in the Earth's crust which allows red-hot magma (molten rock) from the mantle to escape onto the surface of the Earth. An earthquake is a shaking of the ground caused by movements of rocks beneath the Earth's surface.

• See page 6 INSIDE PLANET EARTH for information on the Earth's crust and mantle.

THE CRACKED PLANET

This map shows the edges of the tectonic plates that make up the Earth's surface. The plates are constantly moving by just a few inches each year.

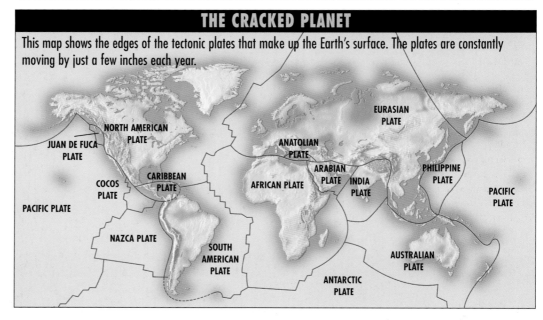

- NORTH AMERICAN PLATE
- JUAN DE FUCA PLATE
- COCOS PLATE
- CARIBBEAN PLATE
- PACIFIC PLATE
- NAZCA PLATE
- SOUTH AMERICAN PLATE
- AFRICAN PLATE
- ANATOLIAN PLATE
- ARABIAN PLATE
- INDIA PLATE
- EURASIAN PLATE
- PHILIPPINE PLATE
- PACIFIC PLATE
- AUSTRALIAN PLATE
- ANTARCTIC PLATE

EVER-CHANGING PLANET

The Earth's tectonic plate movements set off earthquakes and volcanoes, as well as create mountain ranges and deep-sea trenches.

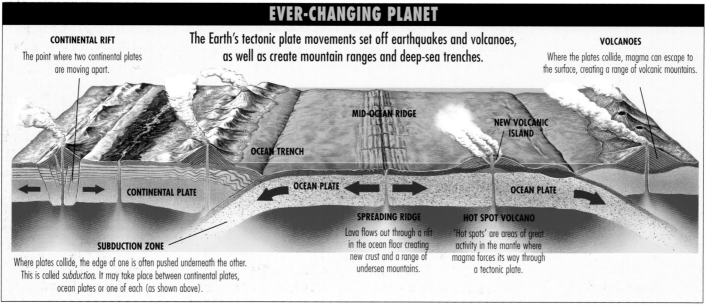

CONTINENTAL RIFT
The point where two continental plates are moving apart.

VOLCANOES
Where the plates collide, magma can escape to the surface, creating a range of volcanic mountains.

MID-OCEAN RIDGE

NEW VOLCANIC ISLAND

OCEAN TRENCH

CONTINENTAL PLATE

OCEAN PLATE

OCEAN PLATE

SPREADING RIDGE
Lava flows out through a rift in the ocean floor creating new crust and a range of undersea mountains.

HOT SPOT VOLCANO
'Hot spots' are areas of great activity in the mantle where magma forces its way through a tectonic plate.

SUBDUCTION ZONE
Where plates collide, the edge of one is often pushed underneath the other. This is called *subduction*. It may take place between continental plates, ocean plates or one of each (as shown above).

STORY OF AN EARTHQUAKE

PLATE MOVEMENTS

Two tectonic plates slowly move, squeezing and stretching the rocks underground. Enormous pressure builds up.

FOCUS OF THE EARTHQUAKE

Miles underground, rocks break and give way, releasing the pressure. The point where this happens is called the *focus* or *hypocenter*.

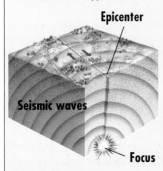

Epicenter

Seismic waves

Focus

SEISMIC WAVES

Vibrations, or *seismic waves*, are sent out from the focus causing the ground at the surface to shake. The point on the surface directly above the focus is called the *epicenter*.

FAULTS

Sometimes, the Earth's crust is put under such pressure that it cracks. The places where the surface cracks open are called *faults*. The lines the cracks create are called *fault lines*.

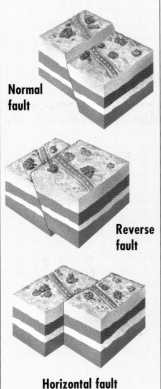

Normal fault

Reverse fault

Horizontal fault

FREQUENCY OF EARTHQUAKES WORLDWIDE

- The magnitude of an earthquake is a measurement of the earthquake's strength and size. The measuring system used here is the Richter Scale.

- The intensity of an earthquake is a measurement of the shaking caused by the earthquake.

Magnitude	Description	Intensity	Average number each year
2 to 2.9	Very minor	Recorded by seismographs, but not felt by people	1,300,000
3 to 3.9	Minor	Felt by some people	130,000
4 to 4.9	Light	Felt by many people	13,000
5 to 5.9	Moderate	Slight damage	1,319
6 to 6.9	Strong	Damaging	134
7 to 7.9	Major	Destructive	17
8 and higher	Great	Devastating	1

INSIDE A VOLCANO

A volcano is a self-made mountain. Its hollow centre provides a pathway between the Earth's upper mantle and the surface.

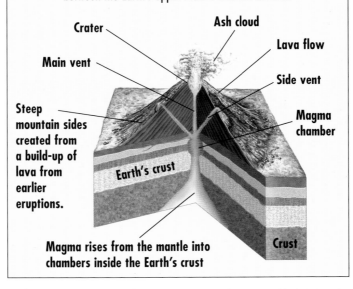

Crater

Ash cloud

Main vent

Lava flow

Side vent

Steep mountain sides created from a build-up of lava from earlier eruptions.

Magma chamber

Earth's crust

Crust

Magma rises from the mantle into chambers inside the Earth's crust

EARTHQUAKE AND VOLCANO DISASTERS

MOST DEADLY EARTHQUAKE

The world's most deadly, recorded earthquake happened in 1556. The earthquake struck in central China. Around 830,000 people were killed when their homes, which were carved in soft rock, collapsed.

KRAKATOA

On August 27, 1883, the volcanic island of Krakatoa, in Indonesia, erupted in a massive explosion which could be heard across 8% of the Earth's surface. Thousands of people were swept out to sea by a giant tsunami caused by the eruption. Over 36,000 people were killed.

EARTHQUAKES IN JAPAN

Japan is situated where four of the Earth's plates meet. In 1923, 143,000 people were killed in the area around Tokyo, Japan's capital, when a magnitude-8.3 earthquake struck. On January 17, 1995, a magnitude-7.2 earthquake killed 5,500 people and destroyed 100,000 homes in Kobe, Japan.

VOLCANO FACTFILE

ACTIVE OR EXTINCT?

Active volcanoes are those that erupt regularly or have the capacity to erupt. They are sometimes called *dormant* if they have not erupted for a very long period. Extinct volcanoes are dead volcanoes. They will not erupt again.

MAGMA/LAVA

Magma is the red-hot, melted rock inside a volcano. As soon as magma leaves a volcano and bursts out into the air or sea, it is known as *lava*. Lava can erupt at temperatures of up to 2192°F.

PLINIAN ERUPTIONS

During a plinian eruption, gas-rich magma explodes inside a volcano. This causes cinder, ash, and gases to be fired up into the air—sometimes as high as 19 miles!

WORLD'S LARGEST VOLCANO

Mauna Loa, Hawaii, is the largest volcano on Earth. Mauna Loa last erupted in 1984.

Mauna Loa's summit is 29,527 feet from the ocean floor. However, scientists estimate that its great mass is actually squashing the ocean floor down by another 26,246 feet, giving the volcano a total height of just under 56,000 feet from seafloor base to summit.

A satellite image of Mauna Loa. The volcano's base spreads over 50% of the island of Hawaii.

Mountains are formed when the Earth's tectonic plates move.

- As layers of rocks push against each other, they buckle and fold at the edges. Mountains are pushed up at upfolds, and valleys are formed in downfolds.

Fold mountain

- When the Earth's crust cracks on a fault, layers of rock on one side of the crack can be pushed up to form a mountain.

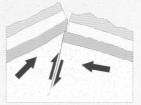

Fault mountain

- When molten magma bursts through the Earth's crust, it hardens and cools, sometimes forming a mountain.

Volcanic mountain

- Heat from molten rock in the mantle pushes layers of solid rock in the Earth's crust upward creating a bulge on the Earth's surface.

Dome mountain

- See page 8
THE CRACKED PLANET and EVER-CHANGING PLANET

MOUNTAINS, LAKES, RIVERS, AND OCEANS

From the Himalayas, the world's tallest mountains, to the deepest ocean trench six and half miles below the surface of the Pacific ocean, the Earth's surface is slowly changing. Mountains grow inch-by-inch and year-by-year, rivers carve new channels as they rush to the sea, and oceans push and pull at the edges of the land.

WORLD'S 10 HIGHEST MOUNTAIN PEAKS

Some mountain peaks stand alone high above the surrounding landscape, but most mountains are joined together to form a range. When several ranges of mountains are grouped together, they are called a *chain*.

The world's ten highest mountain peaks are all in the same range of mountains in Asia — the Himalayas.

Mountain name	Country	Height (feet)
1. Everest	China/Nepal	29,035
2. K2	China/Pakistan	28,251
3. Kanchenjunga	India/Nepal	28,169
4. Lhotse	China/Nepal	27,939
5. Makalu	China/Nepal	27,824
6. Cho Oyu	China/Nepal	26,906
7. Dhaulagiri	Nepal	26,811
8. Manaslu	Nepal	26,758
9. Nanga Parbat	Pakistan	26,660
10. Annapurna	Nepal	26,502

Mount Everest — the highest mountain in the world.

THE ANDES

- The Andes are the world's longest chain of mountains. They stretch down the west coast of South America for around 5,500 miles.

- The Andes include the highest mountain in South America, Aconcagua in Argentina, which is 22,834 feet high. Many of the mountains in the Andes are volcanic.

- The Andes were formed around 70 million years ago by the collision of the Nazca Oceanic Plate with the South American Continental Plate.

WORLD'S 10 LONGEST RIVERS

Rivers begin their lives as small streams high up on mountains or hills. They grow and grow, joining with other small rivers, until they form one big river which reaches the sea or lake. River water comes from rainfall, melted ice or snow, and groundwater from inside the Earth's crust.

River		Length (miles)
1. Nile	Africa	4,144
2. Amazon	South America	4,007
3. Yangtze	Asia	3,964
4. Mississippi-Missouri	N. America	3,740
5. Yenisey-Angara	Asia	3,448
6. Huang He (Yellow)	Asia	3,395
7. Ob-Irtysh	Asia	3,361
8. Congo	Africa	2,900
9. Parana	South America	2,796
10. Mekong	Asia	2,702

(Numbers are rounded as appropriate.)

The Nile River snakes through Egypt's capital city, Cairo. The Nile flows through northeast Africa out into the Mediterranean Sea.

THE WORLD'S OCEANS

There are five oceans in the world and many smaller seas within the oceans.

- The Pacific ocean is the world's largest ocean — its total area is greater than the amount of dry land on Earth.

- The Southern Ocean circumnavigates the continent of Antarctica. It officially became an ocean in 2000, and was formed from the southern sections of the Atlantic, Indian, and Pacific oceans.

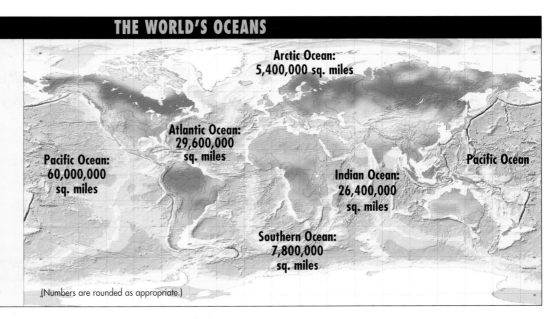

Arctic Ocean:
5,400,000 sq. miles

Atlantic Ocean:
29,600,000 sq. miles

Pacific Ocean:
60,000,000 sq. miles

Pacific Ocean

Indian Ocean:
26,400,000 sq. miles

Southern Ocean:
7,800,000 sq. miles

(Numbers are rounded as appropriate.)

OCEAN DEPTHS AND COASTLINES

The deepest points in each of the world's oceans are listed below. They are measured from *sea level* (the surface of the ocean).

Challenger Deep in the Mariana Trench	Pacific Ocean	-35,840 feet
Milwaukee Deep, Puerto Rico Trench	Atlantic Ocean	-28,232 feet
Java Trench	Indian Ocean	-23,812 feet
Southern end of South Sandwich Trench	Southern Ocean	-23,737 feet
Fram Basin	Arctic Ocean	-15,305 feet

- See page 8 EVER-CHANGING PLANET for information on how ocean trenches are formed.

Total length of coastline on each ocean:

Pacific Ocean	84,297 miles
Atlantic Ocean	69,510 miles
Indian Ocean	41,337 miles
Arctic Ocean	28,203 miles
Southern Ocean	11,165 miles

Coasts can be icy, rocky, or sandy, like these beaches at Rio de Janeiro, Brazil, on South America's east coast.

OCEAN CURRENTS

The oceans are never still. Tides rise and fall, and ocean currents, which are like rivers in oceans, move the water around.

Surface currents are created by the wind. Currents deep underwater are created by temperature differences and the amount of salt in the water.

→ **Warm water currents**
→ **Cold water currents**

WHAT IS A LAKE?

A lake is a large body of water surrounded by land. Most lakes are full of fresh water. Lakes form in basins in the Earth's surface. Rainwater or melted snow and ice collect in the basin. Water also feeds in from rivers and streams.

- Lakes without a river flowing outward lose water through evaporation. The water becomes salty as minerals in the lake become more concentrated. The world's largest lake, the Caspian Sea, is a salt water lake.

- Lake Baykal in Russia is the world's deepest lake. Its deepest point is 5,315 feet deep.

WORLD'S 10 LARGEST LAKES

Lake name		Area (sq. miles)
1. Caspian Sea	Asia	143,244
2. Lake Superior	Canada/USA	31,660
3. Lake Victoria	East Africa	26,641
4. Lake Huron	Canada/USA	23,011
5. Lake Michigan	USA	22,316
6. Lake Tanganyika	Central Africa	12,741
7. Great Bear Lake	Canada	12,084
8. Lake Baykal	Russia	11,969
9. Lake Malawi/Nyasa	East Africa	11,428
10. Aral Sea	Kazakhstan/Uzbekistan	11,076

(Numbers are rounded as appropriate.)

Lake Victoria, the largest lake in Africa. Over 200 species of fish live in its waters.

PHYSICAL WORLD

Planet Earth is three dimensional: it has length, width, and height. In order to create two dimensional maps for an atlas, map makers, called *cartographers*, have devised ways to convert the Earth's curved surface into flat images, called *projections*. The projection below is a physical map of the whole world. It shows physical features such as mountains, and has a key that shows how the map's colors denote different environments, such as tundra and desert.

PHYSICAL MAP OF THE WORLD

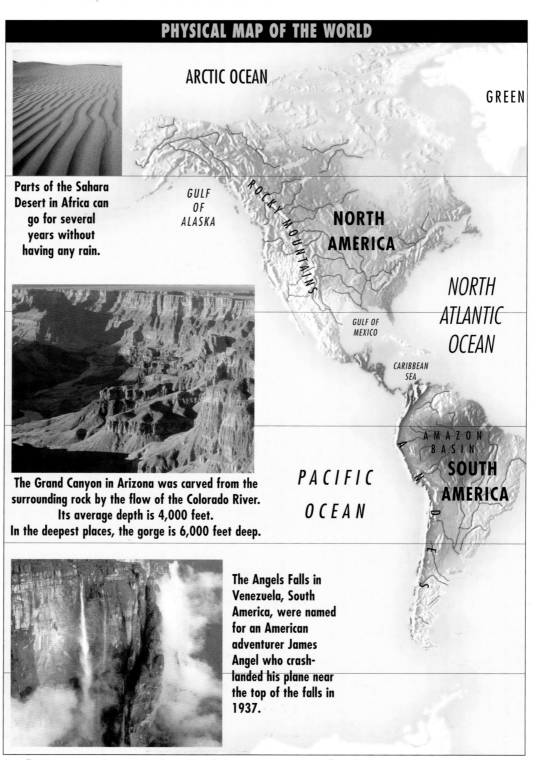

Parts of the Sahara Desert in Africa can go for several years without having any rain.

The Grand Canyon in Arizona was carved from the surrounding rock by the flow of the Colorado River. Its average depth is 4,000 feet. In the deepest places, the gorge is 6,000 feet deep.

The Angels Falls in Venezuela, South America, were named for an American adventurer James Angel who crash-landed his plane near the top of the falls in 1937.

ARCTIC OCEAN

GREEN

GULF OF ALASKA

ROCKY MOUNTAINS

NORTH AMERICA

NORTH ATLANTIC OCEAN

GULF OF MEXICO

CARIBBEAN SEA

AMAZON BASIN

SOUTH AMERICA

ANDES

PACIFIC OCEAN

MAKING MAPS

The projection on these pages was created by a process that's a bit like peeling an orange, then smoothing the skin out.

The flat, peeled version of the Earth was then stretched and manipulated by computer to create the map we see below.

THE CONTINENTS

CONTINENT	Area (square miles)	Percentage of total land
Asia	17,177,000	29.8%
Africa	11,697,000	20.3%
North and Central America	9,357,000	16.2%
South America	6,868,000	11.9%
Antarctica	5,443,000	9.4%
Europe	3,843,000	6.7%
Oceania	3,303,000	5.7%

PHYSICAL MAP OF THE WORLD

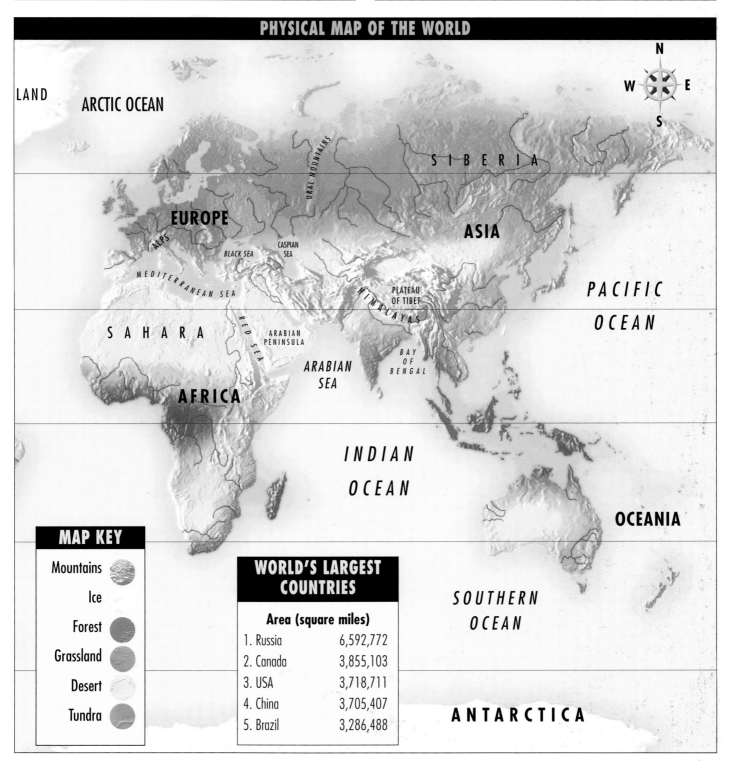

LAND

ARCTIC OCEAN

SIBERIA

EUROPE

ASIA

URAL MOUNTAINS

ALPS

BLACK SEA

CASPIAN SEA

MEDITERRANEAN SEA

PLATEAU OF TIBET

HIMALAYAS

PACIFIC OCEAN

SAHARA

RED SEA

ARABIAN PENINSULA

ARABIAN SEA

BAY OF BENGAL

AFRICA

INDIAN OCEAN

OCEANIA

SOUTHERN OCEAN

ANTARCTICA

MAP KEY

- Mountains
- Ice
- Forest
- Grassland
- Desert
- Tundra

WORLD'S LARGEST COUNTRIES

	Area (square miles)
1. Russia	6,592,772
2. Canada	3,855,103
3. USA	3,718,711
4. China	3,705,407
5. Brazil	3,286,488

POLITICAL WORLD

This map is a political map of the world. The colors on the map show how people divide up the world into territories, or individual countries. The number of countries in the world changes often. Sometimes, large countries divide up into smaller countries. Other times, a group of small countries will join together to become one large country.If you were to look at a political map of the world 50 years from now, it might look quite different to how the political world looks today.

HIGHEST POPULATION BY COUNTRY

1. China	1,306,313,812
2. India	1,080,264,388
3. USA	295,734,134
4. Indonesia	241,973,879
5. Brazil	186,112,794
6. Pakistan	162,419,946
7. Bangladesh	144,319,628
8. Russia	143,420,309
9. Nigeria	128,771,988
10. Japan	127,417,244

POLITICAL MAP OF THE WORLD

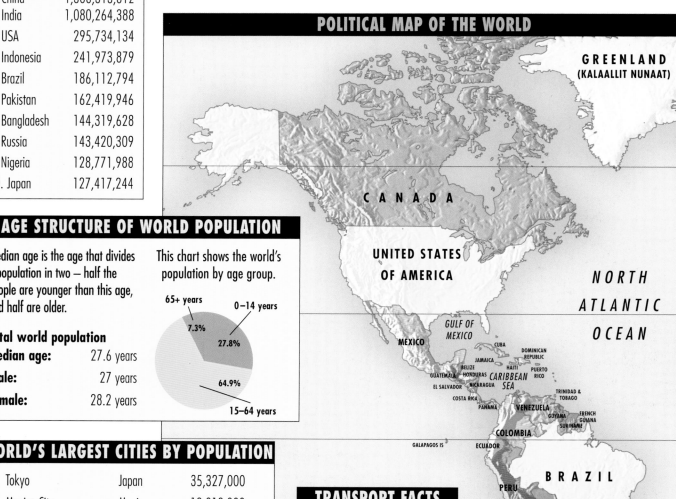

AGE STRUCTURE OF WORLD POPULATION

Median age is the age that divides a population in two – half the people are younger than this age, and half are older.

Total world population	
median age:	27.6 years
Male:	27 years
Female:	28.2 years

This chart shows the world's population by age group.

65+ years 7.3%
0–14 years 27.8%
64.9%
15–64 years

WORLD'S LARGEST CITIES BY POPULATION

1.	Tokyo	Japan	35,327,000
2.	Mexico City	Mexico	19,013,000
3.	New York	USA	18,498,000
4.	Mumbai (Bombay)	India	18,336,000
5.	São Paulo	Brazil	18,333,000
6.	Delhi	India	15,334,000
7.	Kolkata (Calcutta)	India	14,299,000
8.	Buenos Aires	Argentina	13,349,000
9.	Jakarta	Indonesia	13,194,000
10.	Shanghai	China	12,665,000

(Numbers include the city and surrounding urban areas.)

TRANSPORT FACTS

Total length of roads in the world:
20,098,354 miles

Total length of railway in the world:
692,956 miles

Number of airports in the world:
49,973

LIFE EXPECTANCY

Life expectancy at birth total population:
Male: 63 years
Female: 66 years

Highest life expectancy:
Andorra, Europe 83.5 years

Lowest life expectancy:
Botswana, Africa 34 years

• See the GLOSSARY for LIFE EXPECTANCY

WEALTH BY CONTINENT

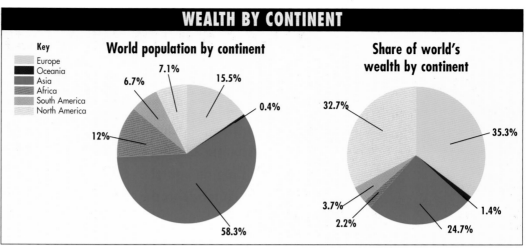

Key
Europe
Oceania
Asia
Africa
South America
North America

World population by continent

7.1%
6.7%
15.5%
0.4%
12%
58.3%

Share of world's wealth by continent

32.7%
35.3%
3.7%
2.2%
24.7%
1.4%

POLITICAL MAP OF THE WORLD

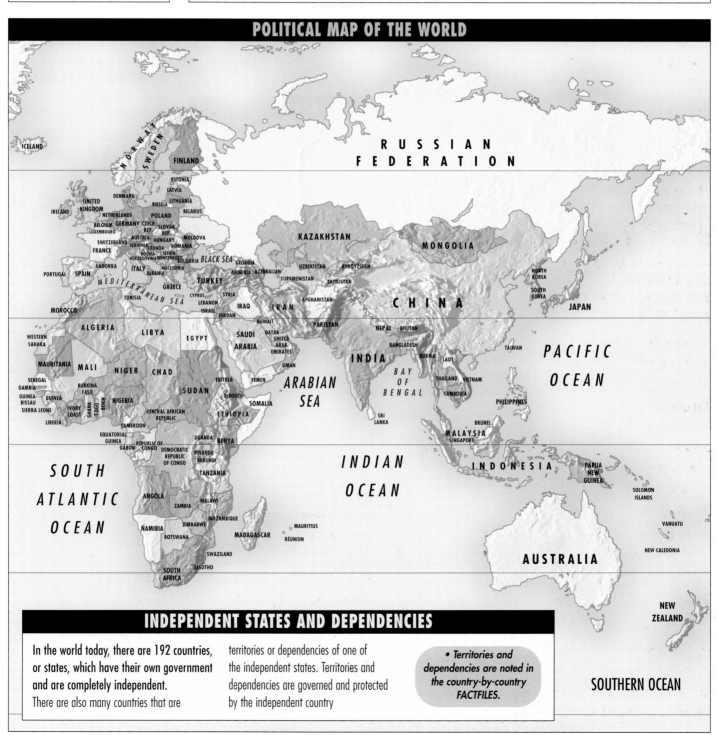

INDEPENDENT STATES AND DEPENDENCIES

In the world today, there are 192 countries, or states, which have their own government and are completely independent.
There are also many countries that are territories or dependencies of one of the independent states. Territories and dependencies are governed and protected by the independent country

• Territories and dependencies are noted in the country-by-country FACTFILES.

SOUTHERN OCEAN

PEOPLE FACTFILE

Total population:
North America: 328,600,000
Central America: 185,800,000

Highest population:
USA 295,734,134

Lowest population:
St. Pierre and Miquelon 7,012

Most populous city:
Mexico City, Mexico
19,013,000 residents

Life expectancy:
North America: 77 years
Central America: 73 years

Highest infant mortality rate:
Haiti: 73 deaths per 1,000 births

• See the GLOSSARY for definitions of LIFE EXPECTANCY and INFANT MORTALITY RATE.

Average annual income per person (in USD):
Highest: USA $40,100
Lowest: Haiti $1,500

GEOGRAPHY FACTFILE

Total land area:
9,357,000 square miles

Largest country:
Canada: 3,855,103 square miles
Second largest country in the world

Smallest country:
Bermuda: 20.5 square miles

Largest lake:
Lake Superior, Canada/USA
Total area: 31,660 square miles

Largest desert:
Great Basin Desert, USA
Total area: 190,000 square miles

Highest waterfall:
Ribbon Fall, Yosemite National Park, USA
Total drop: 1,612 feet

• See page 21 NORTH AMERICA FACTFILES and page 22 CENTRAL AMERICA FACTFILES

The North American continent lies between the Atlantic and Pacific Oceans. This varied region stretches from the icy plains of arctic North America to the hot deserts and lush tropical forests of Central America and the Caribbean islands. Dominating western North America are the Rocky Mountains, which stretch for 3000 miles from Canada to New Mexico, through the United States of America.

Rising majestically from the desert floor, 1000-feet high sandstone rock forms in Monument Valley, Utah.

HIGHEST MOUNTAINS

NAME	LOCATION	HEIGHT (feet)
Mt. McKinley	USA (Alaska)	20,322
Mt. Logan	Canada	19,849
Pico de Orizaba	Mexico	18,406
Mt. St Elias	USA/Canada	18,008

LONGEST RIVERS

NAME	RIVER MOUTH	LENGTH (miles)
Mississippi-Missouri	Gulf of Mexico	3,740
Mackenzie	Arctic Ocean	2,635
Yukon	Pacific Ocean	1,979
Rio Grande	Gulf of Mexico	1,889

LARGEST ISLANDS

NAME	LOCATION	AREA (sq miles)
Greenland	Atlantic Ocean	836,330
Baffin Island	Canada	196,100
Victoria Island	Canada	81,900

• See page 11 WORLD'S 10 LARGEST LAKES

OIL CONSUMPTION

Oil is a fossil fuel (a natural resource) that we burn to produce power for heating and lighting. It is also used as fuel for cars, trucks, and planes.

Oil production and consumption is measured in barrels. A barrel is equivalent to 42 gallons.

TOP 5 CONSUMERS OF OIL (USAGE PER DAY)

USA	19,650,000 barrels
Canada	2,200,000 barrels
Puerto Rico	190,000 barrels
Cuba	163,000 barrels
Jamaica	66,000 barrels

FAST FACTS

• The center of Greenland has sunk to 1,000 feet below sea level due to the weight of the huge ice sheet that covers most of the island.

• At 282 feet below sea level, Death Valley in California is the lowest place in the western hemisphere. Summer temperatures often exceed 120°F.

• The USA is the world's third largest producer of oil—7,800,000 barrels each day.

• The saguaro cactus only grows in the Sonoran desert in the USA and Mexico. Saguaros can grow to 50 feet tall and live for 175 years.

• Cuba is the fifth largest island in the region at 42,803 square miles.

POLITICAL MAP OF NORTH AMERICA

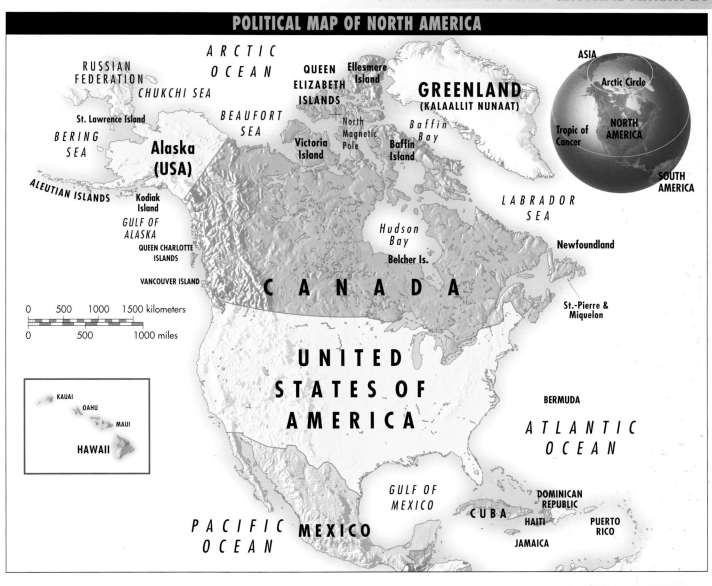

ARCTIC OCEAN

RUSSIAN FEDERATION

CHUKCHI SEA

QUEEN ELIZABETH ISLANDS

Ellesmere Island

GREENLAND (KALAALLIT NUNAAT)

ASIA

Arctic Circle

Tropic of Cancer

NORTH AMERICA

SOUTH AMERICA

St. Lawrence Island

BERING SEA

BEAUFORT SEA

Victoria Island

North Magnetic Pole

Baffin Bay

Baffin Island

Alaska (USA)

ALEUTIAN ISLANDS

Kodiak Island

GULF OF ALASKA

QUEEN CHARLOTTE ISLANDS

VANCOUVER ISLAND

LABRADOR SEA

Hudson Bay

Belcher Is.

Newfoundland

C A N A D A

St.-Pierre & Miquelon

0   500   1000   1500 kilometers
0   500   1000 miles

U N I T E D
S T A T E S   O F
A M E R I C A

KAUAI
OAHU
MAUI
HAWAII

BERMUDA

ATLANTIC OCEAN

GULF OF MEXICO

DOMINICAN REPUBLIC

CUBA

HAITI

PUERTO RICO

PACIFIC OCEAN

MEXICO

JAMAICA

POLITICAL MAP OF CENTRAL AMERICA AND THE CARIBBEAN

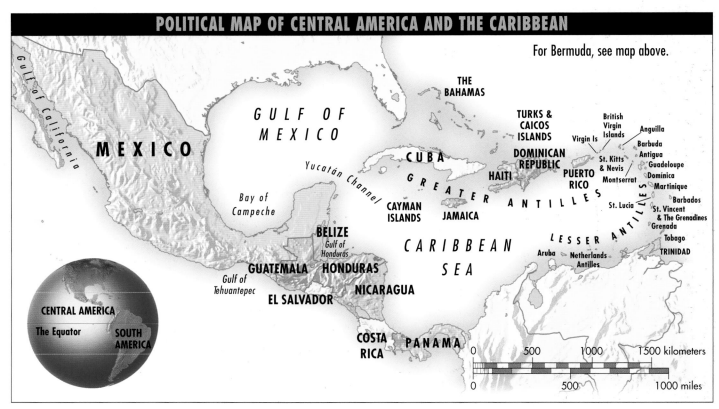

For Bermuda, see map above.

Gulf of California

MEXICO

GULF OF MEXICO

THE BAHAMAS

TURKS & CAICOS ISLANDS

British Virgin Islands

Virgin Is

Anguilla

Barbuda

Antigua

Yucatán Channel

DOMINICAN REPUBLIC

CUBA

St. Kitts & Nevis

Guadeloupe

Dominica

Bay of Campeche

HAITI

PUERTO RICO

Montserrat

Martinique

G R E A T E R   A N T I L L E S

CAYMAN ISLANDS

JAMAICA

St. Lucia

Barbados

St. Vincent & The Grenadines

Grenada

BELIZE
Gulf of Honduras

CARIBBEAN SEA

L E S S E R   A N T I L L E S

Tobago

TRINIDAD

Gulf of Tehuantepec

GUATEMALA

HONDURAS

Aruba

Netherlands Antilles

EL SALVADOR

NICARAGUA

CENTRAL AMERICA

The Equator

SOUTH AMERICA

COSTA RICA

PANAMA

0   500   1000   1500 kilometers
0   500   1000 miles

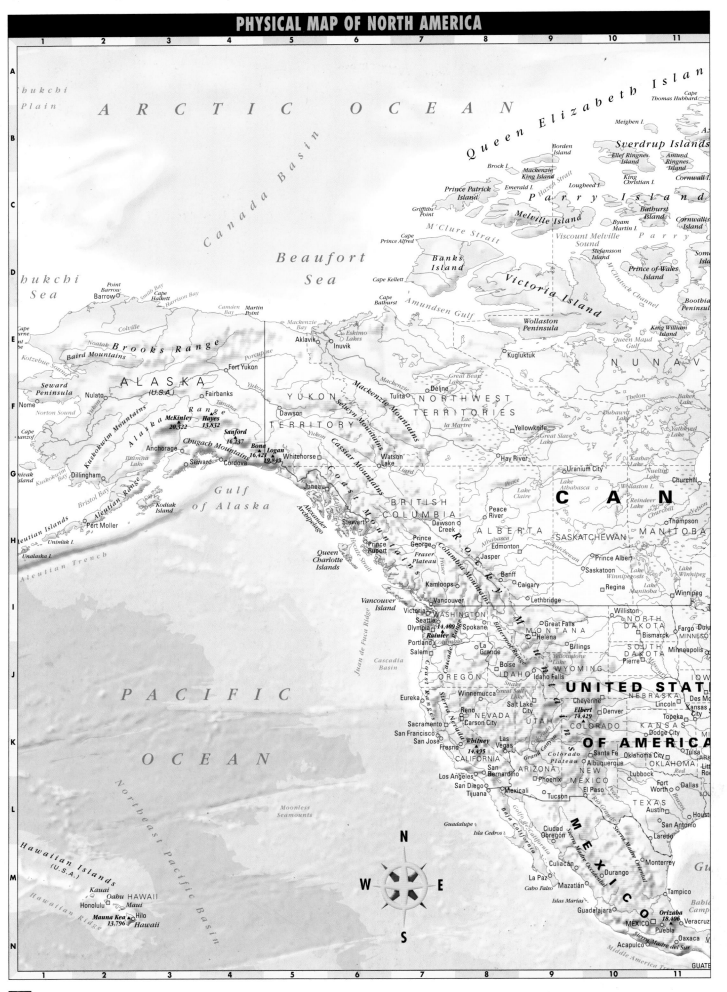

PHYSICAL MAP OF NORTH AMERICA

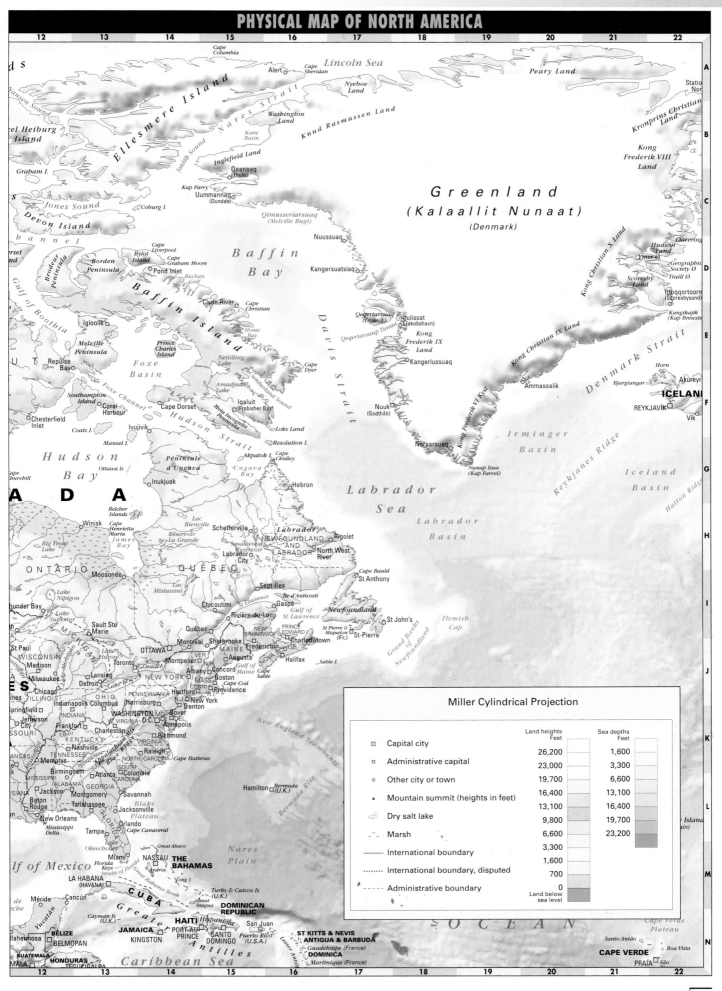

ALT. 0176=° onkeypad

CLIMATE: NORTH AND CENTRAL AMERICA

TEMPERATURES IN JANUARY   **TEMPERATURES IN JULY**

TROPIC OF CANCER   TROPIC OF CANCER

CLIMATES KEY

- over 90° F
- 75° to 90° F
- 60° to 75° F
- 45° to 60° F
- 30° to 45° F
- 15° to 30° F
- 0° to 15° F
- -10° to 0° F
- below -10° F

HABITATS: NORTH AND CENTRAL AMERICA

This map shows the different habitats across the continent.

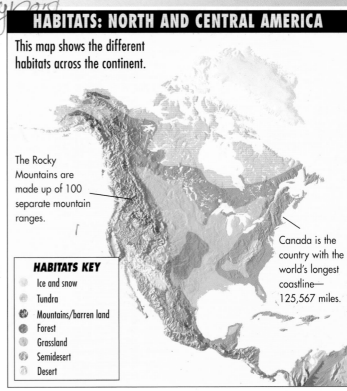

The Rocky Mountains are made up of 100 separate mountain ranges.

Canada is the country with the world's longest coastline— 125,567 miles.

HABITATS KEY

- Ice and snow
- Tundra
- Mountains/barren land
- Forest
- Grassland
- Semidesert
- Desert

LAND USE: NORTH AND CENTRAL AMERICA

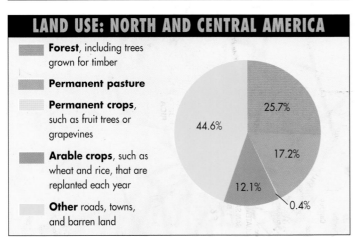

- **Forest**, including trees grown for timber
- **Permanent pasture**
- **Permanent crops**, such as fruit trees or grapevines
- **Arable crops**, such as wheat and rice, that are replanted each year
- **Other** roads, towns, and barren land

25.7%
17.2%
44.6%
12.1%
0.4%

SAN ANDREAS FAULT

The San Andreas fault on the Pacific coast of California, is 746 miles long.
The fault is part of the boundary between the Pacific and North American tectonic plates, and is one of the world's major earthquake zones.

• See page 8 THE CRACKED PLANET

The plates at the San Andreas fault slide past each other at about two inches each year.

NORTH AMERICA FACTFILES

Each country-by-country factfile contains: **total area** of the country in square miles; **total population**; name of the **capital city**; the main **currency** used in the country; **main languages spoken** (listed in order of number of speakers); **top five farming products produced** (listed in order of importance to the country's economy); **natural resources** (of commercial importance); and a country's **status** if it is not independent.

CANADA

Total area (sq. miles): 3,855,103
Total population: 32,805,041
Capital city: Ottawa
Currency: Canadian dollar (CAD)
Languages: English, French
Farming (top 5 products): Wheat, barley, oilseed, tobacco, fruit
Natural resources (top 5): Iron ore, nickel, zinc, copper, gold

GREENLAND
Total area (sq. miles): 836,330
Total population: 56,375
Capital city: Nuuk
Currency: Danish krone (DKK)
Languages: Greenlandic (Inuit mixed with Danish); Danish, English
Farming: Forage crops (for animals), vegetables, sheep, reindeer
Natural resources (top 5): Coal, iron ore, lead, zinc, molybdenum
Status: Self-governing Danish territory

SAINT PIERRE AND MIQUELON
Total area (sq. miles): 93
Total population: 7,012
Capital city: Saint-Pierre
Currency: Euro (EUR)
Languages: Creole
Farming: Vegetables, poultry, livestock
Natural resources: Fish
Status: French overseas territory

UNITED STATES OF AMERICA

Total area (sq. miles): 3,718,711
Total population: 295,734,134
Capital city: Washington DC
Currency: US dollar (USD)
Languages: English, Spanish
Farming (top 5 products): Wheat, corn and other cereal crops, fruit, vegetables, cotton
Natural resources (top 5): Coal, copper, lead, molybdenum, phosphates

• See THE GLOSSARY for words and terms used in these FACTFILES.

• See page 22 CENTRAL AMERICA FACTFILES

CENTRAL AMERICA
FACTFILES

Each country-by-country factfile contains: **total area** of the country in square miles; **total population**; name of the **capital city**; the main **currency** used in the country; **main languages spoken** (listed in order of number of speakers); **top five farming products produced** (listed in order of importance to the country's economy); **natural resources** (of commercial importance; some countries do not have natural resources, such as oil or minerals, but their coastline and climate attract tourists which are vital to the country's economy); and a country's **status** if it is not independent.

An inviting Virgin Islands' beach. For many countries, the beauty of the environment is their most important natural resource.

• See the GLOSSARY for words and terms used in these FACTFILES.

ANGUILLA

Total area (sq. miles): 39
Total population: 13,254
Capital city: The Valley
Currency: East Caribbean dollar (XCD)
Languages: English
Farming: Tobacco, vegetables, cattle
Natural resources: Salt, fish, lobsters
Status: United Kingdom overseas territory

ANTIGUA AND BARBUDA
Total area (sq. miles): 170
Total population: 68,722
Capital city: Saint John's (on Antigua)
Currency: East Caribbean dollar (XCD)
Languages: English, local dialects
Farming (top 5 products): Cotton, vegetables, bananas, coconuts, cucumbers
Natural resources: Limited, but climate good for tourism

ARUBA
Total area (sq. miles): 74.5
Total population: 71,566
Capital city: Oranjestad
Currency: Aruban guilder/florin (AWG)
Languages: Dutch, Papiamento, English
Farming: Aloe plants, livestock
Natural resources: Fish, white sandy beaches that are good for tourism
Status: Self-governing Netherlands territory

BAHAMAS (THE)
Total area (sq. miles): 5382
Total population: 301,790
Capital city: Nassau
Currency: Bahamian dollar (BSD)
Languages: English, Creole
Farming: Citrus fruits, vegetables, poultry
Natural resources: Salt, aragonite, timber

BARBADOS
Total area (sq. miles): 166
Total population: 279,254
Capital city: Bridgetown
Currency: Barbadian dollar (BCD)
Languages: English
Farming: Sugar cane, vegetables, cotton
Natural resources: Oil, fish, natural gas

BELIZE
Total area (sq. miles): 8,867
Total population: 279,457
Capital city: Belmopan
Currency: Belizean dollar (BZD)
Languages: English, Spanish, Mayan
Farming (top 5 products): Bananas, coca, citrus fruits, sugar cane, fish
Natural resources: Timber, fish, hydroelectric power

BERMUDA
Total area (sq. miles): 20.5
Total population: 63,365
Capital city: Hamilton
Currency: Bermudian dollar (BCD)
Languages: English, Portuguese
Farming (top 5 products): Bananas, vegetables, citrus fruits, cut flowers, dairy products
Natural resources: Limestone, climate good for tourism
Status: United Kingdom overseas territory

BRITISH VIRGIN ISLANDS
Total area (sq. miles): 59
Total population: 22,643
Capital city: Road Town
Currency: US dollar (USD)
Languages: English
Farming: Fruit, vegetables, livestock, poultry
Natural resources: Fish, islands good for tourism
Status: United Kingdom overseas territory

CAYMAN ISLANDS
Total area (sq. miles): 101
Total population: 44,270
Capital city: George Town
Currency: Caymanian dollar (KYD)
Languages: English
Farming: Vegetables, fruit, livestock, turtle farming
Natural resources: Fish, climate and beaches good for tourism
Status: United Kingdom overseas territory

COSTA RICA

Total area (sq. miles): 19,730
Total population: 4,016,173
Capital city: San Jose
Currency: Costa Rican colon (CRC)
Languages: Spanish, English
Farming (top 5 products): Coffee, pineapples, bananas, sugar cane, corn
Natural resources: Hydroelectric power

CUBA
Total area (sq. miles): 42,803
Total population: 11,346,670
Capital city: Havana
Currency: Cuban peso (CUP)
Languages: Spanish
Farming (top 5 products): Sugar cane, tobacco, citrus fruits, coffee, rice
Natural resources (top 5): Cobalt, nickel, iron ore, chromium, copper

DOMINICA
Total area (sq. miles): 291
Total population: 69,029
Capital city: Roseau
Currency: East Caribbean dollar (XCD)
Languages: English, French patois
Farming (top 5 products): Bananas, citrus fruits, mangos, root vegetables, coconuts
Natural resources: Timber, hydroelectric power

DOMINICAN REPUBLIC
Total area (sq. miles): 18,815
Total population: 8,950,034
Capital city: Santo Domingo
Currency: Dominican peso (DOP)
Languages: Spanish
Farming (top 5 products): Sugar cane, coffee, cotton, cocoa, tobacco
Natural resources: Nickel, bauxite, gold, silver

EL SALVADOR
Total area (sq. miles): 8,124
Total population: 6,704,932
Capital city: San Salvador
Currency: US dollar (USD)
Languages: Spanish, Nahua
Farming (top 5 products): Coffee, sugar cane, corn, rice, oilseed
Natural resources: Hydroelectric power, geothermal power, oil

GRENADA
Total area (sq. miles): 133
Total population: 89,502
Capital city: Saint George's
Currency: East Caribbean dollar (XCD)
Languages: English, French patois
Farming (top 5 products): Bananas, cocoa, nutmeg, mace, citrus fruits
Natural resources: Timber, tropical fruit, deepwater harbors good for shipping

GUADELOUPE

Total area (sq. miles): 687
Total population: 448,713
Capital city: Basse-Terre
Currency: Euro (EUR)
Languages: French
Farming (top 5 products): Bananas, sugar cane, fruit, vegetables, livestock
Natural resources: Limited, but beaches and climate good for tourism
Status: French overseas territory

GUATEMALA

Total area (sq. miles): 42,043
Total population: 14,655,189
Capital city: Guatemala
Currency: Quetzal (GTQ), US dollar (USD)
Languages: Spanish; Quiche, Cakchiquel, Kekchi, Mam
Farming (top 5 products): Sugar cane, corn, bananas, coffee, beans
Natural resources (top 5): Oil, nickel, timber, fish, chicle

HAITI

Total area (sq. miles): 10,714
Total population: 8,121,622
Capital city: Port-au-Prince
Currency: Gourde (HTG)
Languages: French; Creole
Farming (top 5 products): Coffee, mangos, sugar cane, rice, corn
Natural resources (top 5): Bauxite, copper, calcium carbonate, gold, marble

HONDURAS

Total area (sq. miles): 43,278
Total population: 6,975,204
Capital city: Tegucigalpa
Currency: Lempira (HNL)
Languages: Spanish, Amerindian dialects
Farming (top 5 products): Bananas, coffee, citrus fruits, cattle, timber
Natural resources (top 5): Timber, gold, silver, copper, lead

JAMAICA

Total area (sq. miles): 4,244
Total population: 2,731,832
Capital city: Kingston
Currency: Jamaican dollar (JMD)
Languages: English, English patois
Farming (top 5 products): Sugar cane, bananas, coffee, citrus fruits, yams
Natural resources: Bauxite, gypsum, limestone

MARTINIQUE

Total area (sq. miles): 425
Total population: 432,900
Capital city: Fort-de-France
Currency: Euro (EUR)
Languages: French, Creole patois
Farming (top 5 products): Pineapples, avocados, bananas, cut flowers, vegetables
Natural resources: Limited, but coastline and beaches good for tourism
Status: French overseas territory

MEXICO

Total area (sq. miles): 761,606
Total population: 106,202,903
Capital city: Mexico (Distrito Federal)
Currency: Mexican peso (MXN)
Languages: Spanish, Mayan, Nahuatl
Farming (top 5 products): Corn, wheat, soybeans, rice, beans
Natural resources (top 5): Oil, silver, copper, gold, lead

MONTSERRAT

Total area (sq. miles): 39
Total population: 9,341
Capital city: Temporary government buildings at Brades Estate, Carr's Bay and Little Bay due to 1997 volcano
Currency: East Caribbean dollar (XCD)
Languages: English
Farming (top 5 products): Cabbages, carrots, cucumbers, tomatoes, onions
Natural resources: Very limited
Status: United Kingdom overseas territory

NICARAGUA

Total area (sq. miles): 49,998
Total population: 5,465,100
Capital city: Managua
Currency: Gold cordoba (NIO)
Languages: Spanish
Farming (top 5 products): Coffee, bananas, sugar cane, cotton, rice
Natural resources (top 5): Gold, silver, copper, tungsten, lead

PANAMA

Total area (sq. miles): 30,193
Total population: 3,039,150
Capital city: Panama
Currency: Balboa (PAB), US dollar (USD)
Languages: Spanish, English
Farming (top 5 products): Bananas, rice, corn, coffee, sugar cane
Natural resources: Copper, mahogany forests, shrimps, hydroelectric power

PUERTO RICO

Total area (sq. miles): 3,515
Total population: 3,916,632
Capital city: San Juan
Currency: US dollar (USD)
Languages: Spanish, English
Farming (top 5 products): Sugar cane, coffee, pineapples, plantains, bananas
Natural resources: Copper and nickel (limited amounts), potential for onshore and offshore oil
Status: United States of America Commonwealth

ST. KITTS AND NEVIS

Total area (sq. miles): 101
Total population: 38,958
Capital city: Basseterre
Currency: East Caribbean dollar (XCD)
Languages: English
Farming (top 5 products): Sugar cane, rice, yams, vegetables, bananas
Natural resources: Arable land

ST. LUCIA

Total area (sq. miles): 238
Total population: 166,312
Capital city: Castries
Currency: East Caribbean dollar (XCD)
Languages: English, French patois
Farming (top 5 products): Bananas, coconuts, vegetables, citrus fruits, root vegetables
Natural resources (top 5): Forests, beaches (for tourism), pumice, mineral springs, potential for geothermal power

ST. VINCENT AND THE GRENADINES

Total area (sq. miles): 150
Total population: 117,534
Capital city: Kingstown
Currency: East Caribbean dollar (XCD)
Languages: English; French patois
Farming (top 5 products): Bananas, coconuts, sweet potatoes, spices, livestock
Natural resources: Hydroelectric power

TRINIDAD AND TOBAGO

Total area (sq. miles): 1,980
Total population: 1,088,644
Capital city: Port-of-Spain
Currency: Trinidad and Tobago dollar (TTD)
Languages: English, Hindi, French, Spanish, Chinese
Farming (top 5 products): Cocoa, sugar cane, rice, citrus fruits, coffee
Natural resources: Oil, natural gas, asphalt

TURKS AND CAICOS ISLANDS

Total area (sq. miles): 166
Total population: 20,556
Capital city: Grand Turk
Currency: US dollar (USD)
Languages: English
Farming: Corn, beans, cassava, citrus fruits
Natural resources: Fish, spiny lobsters, conch (tropical marine mollusks)
Status: United Kingdom overseas territory

VIRGIN ISLANDS

Total area (sq. miles): 136
Total population: 108,708
Capital city: Charlotte Amalie
Currency: US dollar (USD)
Languages: English, Spanish or Spanish Creole, French or French Creole
Farming: Fruit, vegetables, sorghum, cattle
Natural resources: Limited, but climate and beaches good for tourism
Status: United States unincorporated territory

Opened in 1914, the 50-mile-long, man-made Panama Canal allows ships to sail from the Pacific Ocean to the Atlantic Ocean. Before the canal was built, ships had to sail all the way around South America by Cape Horn.

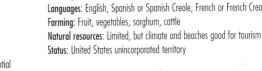

SOUTH AMERICA

The Amazon River accounts for twenty percent of all freshwater that drains into the world's oceans each year.

The continent of South America stretches from the warm waters of the Caribbean Sea in the north to the stormy, cold waters of Cape Horn in the south. The world's longest mountain chain, the Andes, runs down the western coast, while the dense, dark Amazon forest, the world's largest rainforest, spreads across the north of the continent.

PEOPLE FACTFILE

Total population:
371,400,000

Highest population:
Brazil 186,112,794

Lowest population:
Paraguay 6,347,884

Most populous city:
São Paulo, Brazil
18,333,000 residents

Life expectancy:
Male: 70 years
Female: 76 years

Highest infant mortality rate:
Bolivia: 53 deaths per 1,000 births

• See the GLOSSARY for definitions of LIFE EXPECTANCY and INFANT MORTALITY RATE.

Average annual income per person (in USD):
Highest: Uruguay $14,500
Lowest: Bolivia $2,600

GEOGRAPHY FACTFILE

Total land area:
6,868,000 square miles

Largest country:
Brazil: 3,286,488 square miles
Fifth largest country in the world

Smallest country:
Netherlands Antilles:
371 square miles

Largest island:
Isla Grande de Tierra del Fuego
18,147 square miles

Largest desert:
Atacama Desert, Chile
31,000 square miles
There has never been any rainfall recorded in parts of this desert.

Highest waterfall:
Angel Falls, Venezuela
Total drop: 3,212 feet

• See page 27
SOUTH AMERICA FACTFILES

HIGHEST MOUNTAINS (BY COUNTRY)

NAME	LOCATION	HEIGHT (feet)
Aconcagua	Argentina	22,834*
Ojos del Salado	Argentina/Chile	22,664
Huascaran	Peru	22,205
Sajama	Bolivia	21,463
Chimborazo	Ecuador	20,702

* Aconcagua is the highest mountain in South America.

• See page 10 THE ANDES

LONGEST RIVERS

NAME	RIVER MOUTH	LENGTH (miles)
Amazon	Atlantic Ocean	4,007
Parana	Atlantic Ocean	2,796
Purus	Amazon	2,082
Madeira	Amazon	1,988

LARGEST LAKES

NAME	LOCATION	AREA (sq miles)
Lake Titicaca	Bolivia/Peru	3,205
Lake Poopo	Bolivia	1,081

HABITATS

This map shows the different types of habitats across the continent.

KEY
- Ice and snow
- Tundra
- Mountains/barren land
- Forest
- Grassland
- Semidesert
- Desert

AMAZON RAINFOREST FACTS

Rainforests around the world are shrinking. They are cut down by the timber industry or cleared for mineral mining and farming.

- Just 2.5 acres of Amazon rainforest can contain up to 1500 different plant species. Each species of tree may support more than 400 different insect species.

- 20% of the world's birds live in the Amazon rainforest.

- 500 years ago, 6 million native people lived in the Amazon rainforest. In 2000, the number was less than 250,000.

FAST FACTS

- Venezuela is South America's main producer of oil. Brazil uses the most oil in South America, 2,199,000 barrels each day.

- The Amazon's source is a remote slope of the Nevado Mismi peak (17,440 feet high), in Peru.

- La Paz in Bolivia is the world's highest capital city, about 12,000 feet above sea level.

POLITICAL MAP OF SOUTH AMERICA

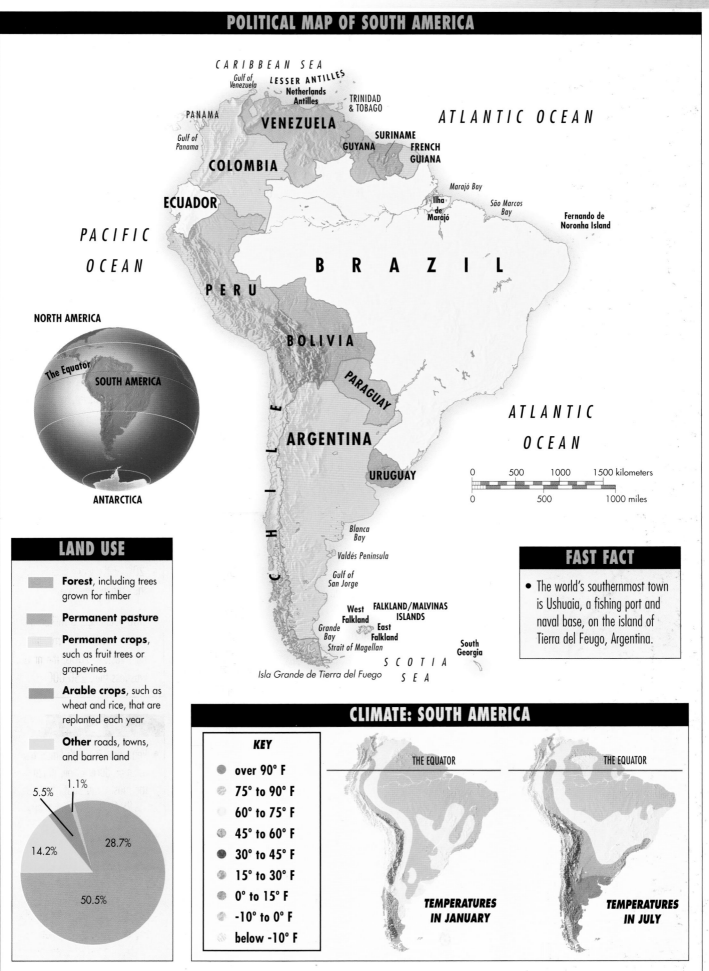

CARIBBEAN SEA
Gulf of Venezuela
LESSER ANTILLES
Netherlands Antilles
TRINIDAD & TOBAGO
ATLANTIC OCEAN
PANAMA
VENEZUELA
Gulf of Panama
GUYANA
SURINAME
FRENCH GUIANA
COLOMBIA
ECUADOR
Marajó Bay
Ilha de Marajó
São Marcos Bay
Fernando de Noronha Island
PACIFIC OCEAN
BRAZIL
PERU
NORTH AMERICA
The Equator
SOUTH AMERICA
BOLIVIA
ANTARCTICA
PARAGUAY
ARGENTINA
ATLANTIC OCEAN
URUGUAY
CHILE
Blanca Bay
Valdés Peninsula
Gulf of San Jorge
West Falkland
FALKLAND/MALVINAS ISLANDS
Grande Bay
East Falkland
Strait of Magellan
South Georgia
Isla Grande de Tierra del Fuego
SCOTIA SEA

0 500 1000 1500 kilometers
0 500 1000 miles

LAND USE

Forest, including trees grown for timber

Permanent pasture

Permanent crops, such as fruit trees or grapevines

Arable crops, such as wheat and rice, that are replanted each year

Other roads, towns, and barren land

1.1%
5.5%
14.2%
28.7%
50.5%

FAST FACT

- The world's southernmost town is Ushuaia, a fishing port and naval base, on the island of Tierra del Feugo, Argentina.

CLIMATE: SOUTH AMERICA

KEY

- over 90° F
- 75° to 90° F
- 60° to 75° F
- 45° to 60° F
- 30° to 45° F
- 15° to 30° F
- 0° to 15° F
- -10° to 0° F
- below -10° F

THE EQUATOR

THE EQUATOR

TEMPERATURES IN JANUARY

TEMPERATURES IN JULY

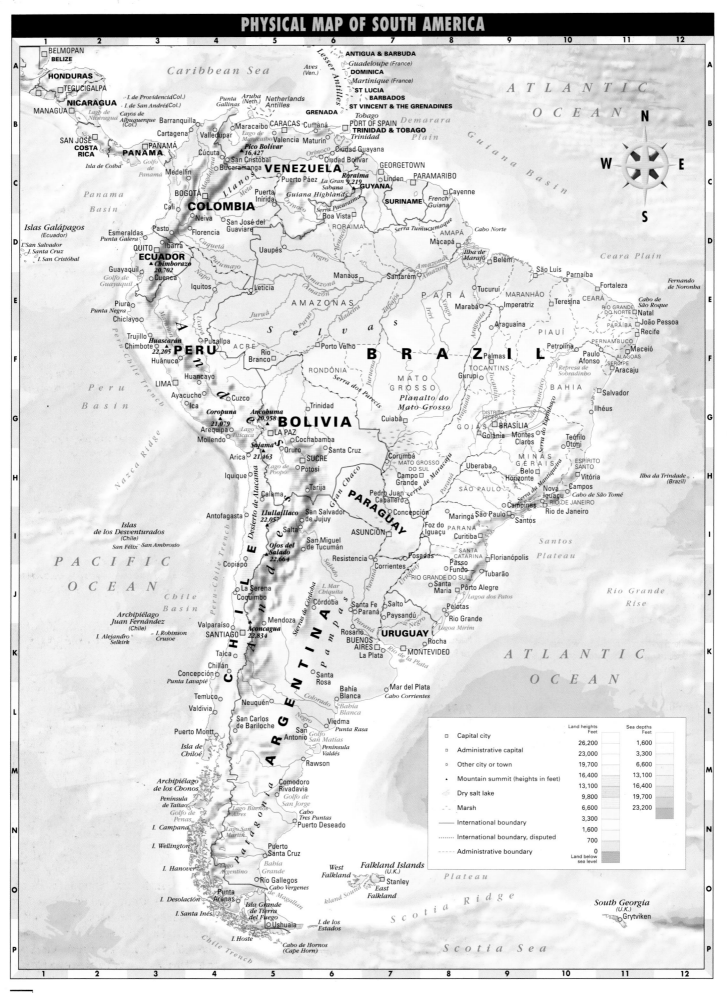

PHYSICAL MAP OF SOUTH AMERICA

Caribbean Sea

ATLANTIC OCEAN

BELMOPAN
BELIZE
HONDURAS
TEGUCIGALPA
NICARAGUA
MANAGUA
Lago de Nicaragua
SAN JOSÉ
COSTA RICA
PANAMÁ
PANAMA
Isla de Coiba
Golfo de Panamá
Panama Basin

ANTIGUA & BARBUDA
Guadeloupe (France)
DOMINICA
Martinique (France)
ST LUCIA
BARBADOS
ST VINCENT & THE GRENADINES
GRENADA
Aves (Ven.)
Lesser Antilles

Tobago
PORT OF SPAIN
TRINIDAD & TOBAGO
Trinidad
Demarara Plain

Guiana Basin

I. de Providencia(Col.)
I. de San Andrés(Col.)
Cayos de Albuquerque (Col.)
Barranquilla
Cartagena
Maracaibo
Valledupar
Lago de Maracaibo
Punta Gallinas
Netherlands Antilles
Aruba (Neth.)
CARACAS
Cumaná
Maturín
Valencia
Ciudad Guayana
Orinoco
Ciudad Bolívar
GEORGETOWN
Linden
PARAMARIBO
Cayenne
French Guiana

Cúcuta
San Cristóbal
Bucaramanga
Pico Bolívar 16,427
VENEZUELA
Puerto Páez
Roraima 9,219
La Gran Sabana
GUYANA
SURINAME

Medellín
BOGOTÁ
Cali
Puerto Inírida
Serra Pacaraima
Boa Vista
RORAIMA
Serra Tumucumaque
Cabo Norte
AMAPÁ
Macapá

Llanos
Meta
Guiana Highlands
Serra Parima

Esmeraldas
Punta Galera
Pasto
Neiva
Florencia
San José del Guaviare
COLOMBIA
Caquetá
Uaupés
Branco
Negro
Ilha de Marajó
Belém
São Luís
Parnaíba
Ceara Plain
Fernando de Noronha

Islas Galápagos (Ecuador)
I.San Salvador
I. Santa Cruz
I. San Cristóbal
QUITO
Ibarra
ECUADOR
Chimborazo 20,702
Cuenca
Guayaquil
Golfo de Guayaquil
Patumayo
Napo
Iquitos
Leticia
Manaus
Santarém
Amazonas
Amazon
PARÁ
Tucuruí
Marabá
Imperatriz
Teresina
CEARÁ
Fortaleza
Cabo de São Roque
Natal
João Pessoa
Recife
Maceió

Piura
Punta Negra
Chiclayo
Trujillo
Chimbote
Huascarán 22,205
Huánuco
PERU
Juruá
Pucallpa
Río Branco
ACRE
Porto Velho
RONDÔNIA
Serra dos Parecis
BRAZIL
MATO GROSSO
Gurupi
Palmas
TOCANTINS
MARANHÃO
PIAUÍ
PERNAMBUCO
ALAGOAS
SERGIPE
Petrolina
Rio São Francisco
Aracaju
Represa de Sobradinho
BAHIA
Salvador
Ilhéus

Peru Basin
Amazon
Selvas
Madeira
Tapajós
Xingu
Araguaia
Tocantins

Lima
Huancayo
Ayacucho
Ica
Cuzco
Coropuna 21,079
Arequipa
Ancohuma 20,958
BOLIVIA
LA PAZ
Cochabamba
Santa Cruz
Trinidad
Cuiabá
Planalto do Mato Grosso
GOIÁS
BRASÍLIA
DISTRITO FEDERAL
Goiânia
Montes Claros
MINAS GERAIS
Teófilo Otoni
ESPÍRITO SANTO
Belo Horizonte
Vitória
Ilha da Trindade (Brazil)

Nazca Ridge
Peru-Chile Trench
Sajama 21,463
Mollendo
Arica
Lago Titicaca
Oruro
SUCRE
Potosí
Lago de Poopó
Tarija
Corumbá
MATO GROSSO DO SUL
Campo Grande
SÃO PAULO
Uberaba
Uberlândia
Nova Iguaçu
Campos
Cabo de São Tomé
Campinas
São Paulo
RIO DE JANEIRO
Rio de Janeiro
Santos
Serra da Mantiqueira

Iquique
Calama
Antofagasta
Llullaillaco 22,057
Salta
San Salvador de Jujuy
PARAGUAY
Pedro Juan Caballero
Concepción
ASUNCIÓN
Maringá
PARANÁ
Curitiba
SANTA CATARINA
Florianópolis
Santos Plateau

Desierto de Atacama
Gran Chaco
Serra de Maracaju
Paraná
Foz do Iguaçu

Islas de los Desventurados (Chile)
San Félix
San Ambrosio
Ojos del Salado 22,664
Copiapó
San Miguel de Tucumán
Resistencia
Corrientes
Posadas
RIO GRANDE DO SUL
Passo Fundo
Tubarão
Santa Maria
Pôrto Alegre
Rio Grande Rise

PACIFIC OCEAN
Chile Basin
La Serena
Coquimbo
L. Mar Chiquita
Córdoba
Santa Fe
Paraná
Salto
Paysandú
Santa
Pelotas
Rio Grande
Lagoa dos Patos

Archipiélago Juan Fernández (Chile)
I. Alejandro Selkirk
I. Robinson Crusoe
Valparaíso
Aconcagua 22,834
SANTIAGO
Mendoza
Rosario
BUENOS AIRES
La Plata
URUGUAY
MONTEVIDEO
Rocha
Río de la Plata
Negro
Lagoa Mirim

Talca
Sierras de Córdoba
ARGENTINA
Pampas
Santa Rosa
Mar del Plata

Chillán
Concepción
Punta Lavapié
Neuquén
Bahía Blanca
Bahía Blanca
Cabo Corrientes

ATLANTIC OCEAN

Temuco
Valdivia
Puerto Montt
San Carlos de Bariloche
San Antonio
Viedma
Punta Rasa
Colorado
Negro
Golfo San Matías
Península Valdés

Isla de Chiloé
Rawson
Comodoro Rivadavia
Golfo de San Jorge

Archipiélago de los Chonos
Península de Taitao
Golfo de Penas
I. Campana
Lago Buenos Aires
Lago San Martín
Cabo Tres Puntas
Puerto Deseado

I. Wellington
Puerto Santa Cruz
Bahía Grande
Falkland Islands (U.K.)
West Falkland
Stanley
East Falkland
Plateau

I. Hanover
Río Gallegos
Cabo Vírgenes
Isla Grande de Tierra del Fuego
Bahía Argentino
kland Sound
Scotia Ridge
South Georgia (U.K.)
Grytviken

Patagonia
Estrecho de Magallanes

I. Desolación
I. Santa Inés
Punta Arenas
Ushuaia
I. de los Estados
Cabo de Hornos (Cape Horn)
I. Hoste
Chile Trench
Scotia Sea

Legend

Symbol	Description	Land heights Feet	Sea depths Feet
□	Capital city	26,200	1,600
□	Administrative capital	23,000	3,300
○	Other city or town	19,700	6,600
▲	Mountain summit (heights in feet)	16,400	13,100
	Dry salt lake	13,100	16,400
	Marsh	9,800	19,700
		6,600	23,200
	International boundary	3,300	
	International boundary, disputed	1,600	
	Administrative boundary	700	
		0	
		Land below sea level	

SOUTH AMERICA FACTFILES

Each country-by-country factfile contains: **total area** of the country in square miles; **total population**; name of the **capital city**; the main **currency** used in the country; **main languages spoken** (listed in order of number of speakers); **top five farming products produced** (listed in order of importance to the country's economy); **natural resources** (of commercial importance); and a country's **status** if it is not independent.

ARGENTINA

Total area (sq. miles): 1,068,302
Total population: 39,537,943
Capital city: Buenos Aires
Currency: Argentine peso (ARS)
Languages: Spanish, English, Italian, German, French
Farming (top 5 products): Sunflower seeds, lemons, soybeans; grapes, corn
Natural resources (top 5): Fertile pampas plains, lead, zinc, tin, copper

BOLIVIA
Total area (sq. miles): 424,164
Total population: 8,857,870
Capital city: La Paz/Sucre
Currency: Boliviano (BOB)
Languages: Spanish, Quechua, Aymara
Farming (top 5 products): Soybeans, coffee, coca, cotton, corn
Natural resources (top 5): Tin, natural gas, oil, zinc, tungsten

BRAZIL
Total area (sq. miles): 3,286,488
Total population: 186,112,794
Capital city: Brasilia
Currency: Real (BRL)
Languages: Portuguese, Spanish, English, French
Farming (top 5 products): Coffee, soybeans, wheat, rice, corn
Natural resources (top 5): Bauxite, gold, iron ore, manganese, nickel

CHILE
Total area (sq. miles): 292,260
Total population: 15,980,912
Capital city: Santiago
Currency: Chilean peso (CLP)
Languages: Spanish
Farming (top 5 products): Fruit, onions, wheat, corn, oats
Natural resources (top 5): Copper, timber, iron ore, nitrates, precious metals

COLOMBIA
Total area (sq. miles): 439,736
Total population: 42,954,279
Capital city: Bogota
Currency: Colombian peso (COP)
Languages: Spanish
Farming (top 5 products): Coffee, cut flowers, bananas, rice, tobacco
Natural resources (top 5): Oil, natural gas, coal, iron ore, nickel

ECUADOR
Total area (sq. miles): 109,483
Total population: 13,363,593
Capital city: Quito
Currency: US dollar (USD)
Languages: Spanish, Quechua
Farming (top 5 products): Bananas, coffee, cocoa, rice, potatoes
Natural resources (top 5): Oil, fish, timber, hydroelectric power

FRENCH GUIANA
Total area (sq. miles): 35,135
Total population: 195,506
Capital city: Cayenne
Currency: Euro (EUR)
Languages: French
Farming (top 5 products): Corn, rice, manioc (tapioca), sugar cane, cocoa
Natural resources (top 5): Bauxite, timber, gold, oil, kaolin
Status: French overseas territory

GUYANA
Total area (sq. miles): 83,000
Total population: 765,283
Capital city: Georgetown
Currency: Guyanese dollar (GYD)
Languages: English, Amerindian dialects, Creole, Hindi
Farming (top 5 products): Sugar cane, rice, wheat, vegetable oils, livestock
Natural resources (top 5): Bauxite, gold, diamonds, timber, shrimp

NETHERLANDS ANTILLES
Total area (sq. miles): 371
Total population: 219,958
Capital city: Willestad
Currency: Netherlands Antillean guilder (ANG)
Languages: Papiamento, English, Dutch
Farming (top 5 products): Aloe plants, sorghum, peanuts, vegetables, tropical fruit
Natural resources: Phosphates (on Curacao island), salt (on Bonaire island)
Status: Self-governing Netherlands territory

PARAGUAY

Total area (sq. miles): 157,047
Total population: 6,347,884
Capital city: Asuncion
Currency: Guarani (PYG)
Languages: Spanish, Guarani
Farming (top 5 products): Cotton, sugar cane, soybeans, corn, wheat
Natural resources (top 5): Hydroelectric power, timber, iron ore, manganese, limestone

PERU

Total area (sq. miles): 496,226
Total population: 27,925,628
Capital city: Lima
Currency: Nuevo sol (PEN)
Languages: Spanish; Quechua; Aymara
Farming (top 5 products): Coffee, cotton, sugar cane, rice, potatoes
Natural resources (top 5): Copper, silver, gold, oil, timber

SURINAME
Total area (sq. miles): 63,039
Total population: 438,144
Capital city: Paramaribo
Currency: Suriname guilder (SRG)
Languages: Dutch, English, Sranang Tongo (Creole language sometimes called *Taki-Taki*)
Farming (top 5 products): Rice, bananas, palm kernels, coconuts, plantains
Natural resources (top 5): Timber, hydroelectric power, fish, kaolin, shrimp

URUGUAY
Total area (sq. miles): 68,038
Total population: 3,415,920
Capital city: Montevideo
Currency: Uruguayan peso (UYU)
Languages: Spanish
Farming (top 5 products): Rice, wheat, corn, barley, livestock
Natural resources: Hydroelectric power, minerals, fish

VENEZUELA
Total area (sq. miles): 352,144
Total population: 25,375,281
Capital city: Caracas
Currency: Bolivar (VEB)
Languages: Spanish, numerous indigenous dialects
Farming (top 5 products): Corn, sorghum, sugar cane, rice, bananas
Natural resources (top 5): Oil, natural gas, iron ore, gold, bauxite

• See the GLOSSARY for words and terms used in these FACTFILES.

Llamas are members of the camel family and are native to South America. They have lived in the Andes for centuries, both as wild animals and in domesticated herds. Today, they still work as pack animals carrying goods through inaccessible mountain passes.

GEOGRAPHY FACTFILE

Total land area:
11,697,000 square miles

Largest country:
Sudan: 967,499 square miles

Smallest country:
Mayotte: 144 square miles

Largest lake:
Lake Victoria, East Africa
26,641 square miles

Largest desert:
Sahara Desert, North Africa
3.5 million square miles
Largest desert in the world

Highest waterfall:
Tugela Falls, South Africa
Total drop: 3,110 feet

• See page 33
AFRICA FACTFILES

AFRICA

Africa is the second largest continent in the world. The world's biggest desert, the Sahara, dominates the landscape of the north, while in the south forests and vast grasslands are home to wild animals, such as leopards, lions, and elephants. The Great Rift Valley, one of the Earth's major geological features, runs from the Red Sea down to Mozambique. This huge crack in the Earth's surface, caused by a series of faults, is made up of mountains, volcanoes, deep valleys, and lakes.

An African leopard in the
Samburu Game Reserve, Kenya.

HIGHEST MOUNTAINS

NAME	LOCATION	HEIGHT (feet)
Mt. Kilimanjaro	Tanzania	19,341
Mt. Kirinyaga (Mt. Kenya)	Kenya	17,060
Mount Stanley (Margherita Peak)	Dem. Rep. Congo/Uganda	16,765
Ras Dashen	Ethiopia	15,157

LONGEST RIVERS

NAME	RIVER MOUTH	LENGTH (miles)
Nile	Mediterranean	4,144
Congo	Atlantic Ocean	2,900
Niger	Atlantic Ocean	2,597
Zambezi	Indian Ocean	2,200

LARGEST ISLANDS

NAME		AREA (sq miles)
Madagascar	Indian Ocean	226,657
Réunion	Indian Ocean	972

• See page 11 WORLD'S 10 LARGEST LAKES

OIL CONSUMPTION

The amount of oil produced, bought and sold, and used in the world is measured in barrels. A barrel is equivalent to 42 gallons.

Nigeria is Africa's largest producer of oil — 2,356,000 barrels per day

TOP 5 CONSUMERS OF OIL (USAGE PER DAY)	
Egypt	562,000 barrels
South Africa	460,000 barrels
Nigeria	275,000 barrels
Libya	216,000 barrels
Algeria	209,000 barrels

FAST FACTS

• Almost 90% of the rainforest in West Africa has been destroyed.

• 90% of the rainforest on the African island of Madagascar has been destroyed. Around 80% of the animal species found on Madagascar live only on this island and nowhere else on Earth (other than zoo populations).

• See page 24
AMAZON RAINFOREST FACTS

• Namibia was the first country in the world to include protecting the environment in its constitution. Around 14% of Namibia is now protected including the entire Namib Desert coast.

• Ancient rock paintings show that 8,000 years ago the Sahara Desert was a lush, green place that was home to many wild animals.

• It is believed that the first place in the world to cultivate coffee was Ethiopia. It was grown in the Kefa region of Ethiopia around 1000 years ago.

POLITICAL MAP OF AFRICA

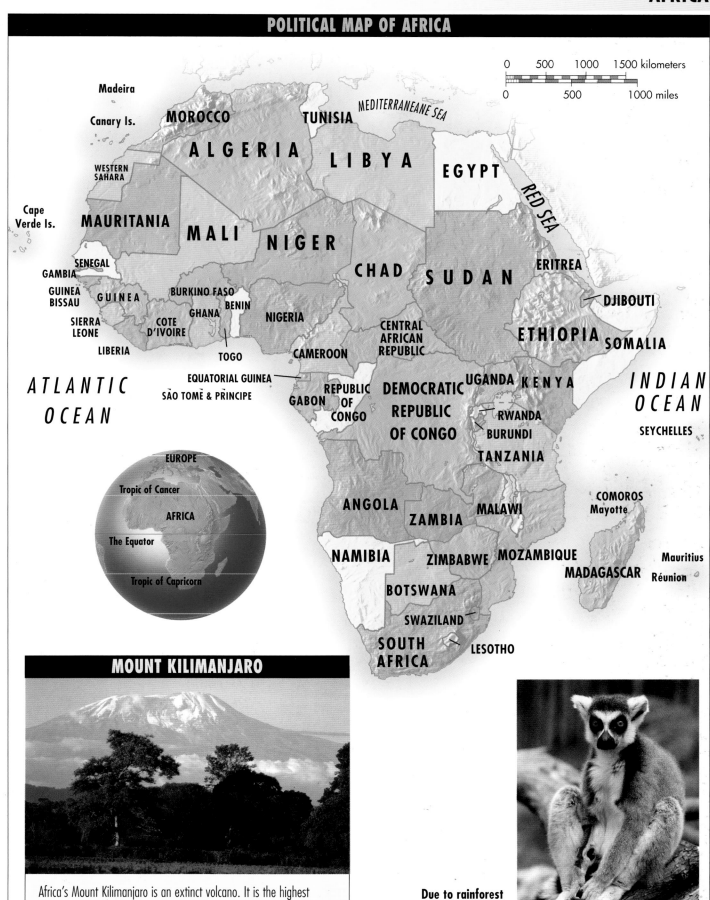

0   500   1000   1500 kilometers

0   500   1000 miles

Madeira

Canary Is.

MOROCCO

TUNISIA

MEDITERRANEANE SEA

ALGERIA

LIBYA

EGYPT

WESTERN SAHARA

RED SEA

Cape Verde Is.

MAURITANIA

MALI

NIGER

CHAD

SUDAN

ERITREA

SENEGAL

DJIBOUTI

GAMBIA

GUINEA BISSAU

GUINEA

BURKINO FASO

BENIN

ETHIOPIA

SOMALIA

GHANA

NIGERIA

SIERRA LEONE

COTE D'IVOIRE

CENTRAL AFRICAN REPUBLIC

LIBERIA

TOGO

CAMEROON

ATLANTIC OCEAN

EQUATORIAL GUINEA

SÃO TOMÉ & PRINCIPE

REPUBLIC OF CONGO

GABON

DEMOCRATIC REPUBLIC OF CONGO

UGANDA

KENYA

RWANDA

BURUNDI

INDIAN OCEAN

TANZANIA

SEYCHELLES

EUROPE

Tropic of Cancer

AFRICA

The Equator

ANGOLA

ZAMBIA

MALAWI

COMOROS

Mayotte

Tropic of Capricorn

NAMIBIA

ZIMBABWE

MOZAMBIQUE

Mauritius

MADAGASCAR

Réunion

BOTSWANA

SWAZILAND

SOUTH AFRICA

LESOTHO

MOUNT KILIMANJARO

Africa's Mount Kilimanjaro is an extinct volcano. It is the highest mountain in the world that it is possible to scale without special climbing skills or equipment. Around 22,000 people climb Kilimanjaro every year, making it the world's most climbed mountain.

Due to rainforest destruction, many Madagascan animals, such as this ring-tailed lemur, are endangered.

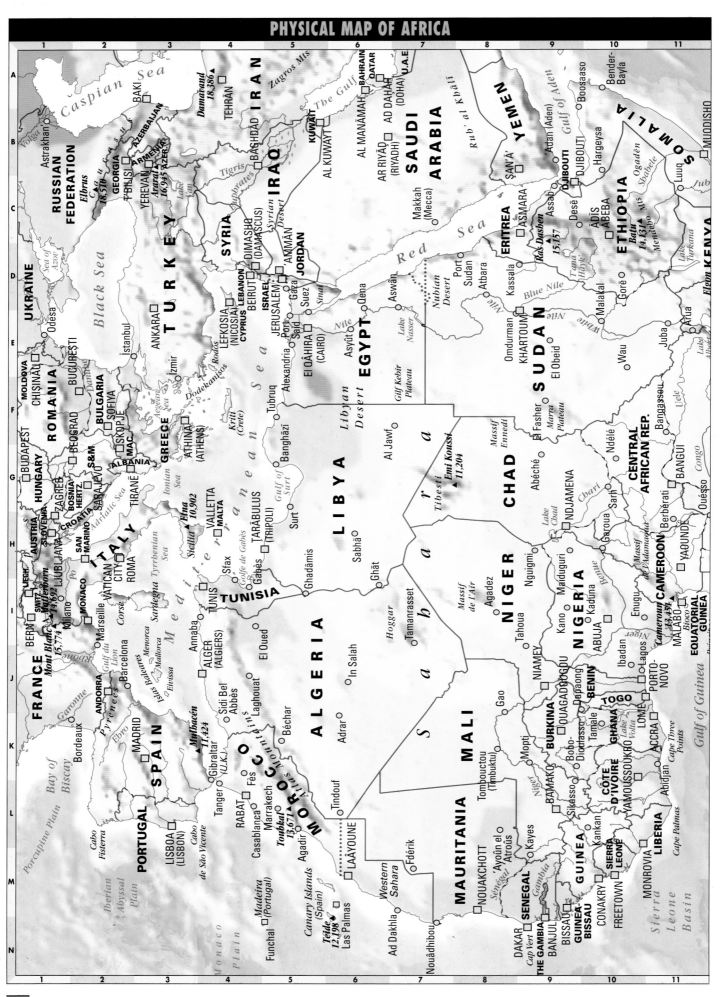

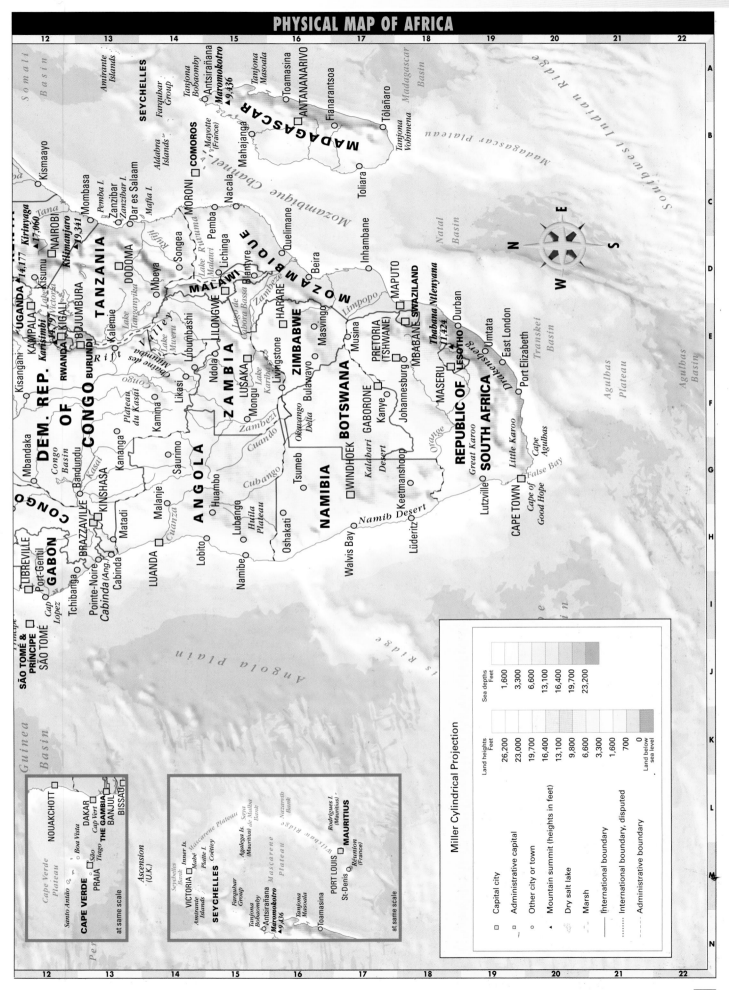

HABITATS AND PROTECTING AFRICA'S WILDLIFE

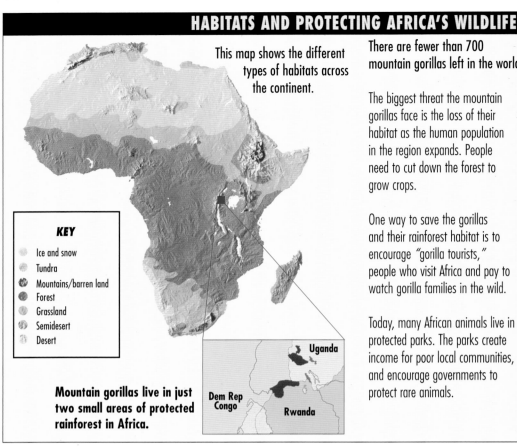

This map shows the different types of habitats across the continent.

KEY
- Ice and snow
- Tundra
- Mountains/barren land
- Forest
- Grassland
- Semidesert
- Desert

Mountain gorillas live in just two small areas of protected rainforest in Africa.

Uganda

Dem Rep Congo

Rwanda

There are fewer than 700 mountain gorillas left in the world.

The biggest threat the mountain gorillas face is the loss of their habitat as the human population in the region expands. People need to cut down the forest to grow crops.

One way to save the gorillas and their rainforest habitat is to encourage "gorilla tourists," people who visit Africa and pay to watch gorilla families in the wild.

Today, many African animals live in protected parks. The parks create income for poor local communities, and encourage governments to protect rare animals.

CLIMATE: AFRICA

TEMPERATURES IN JANUARY

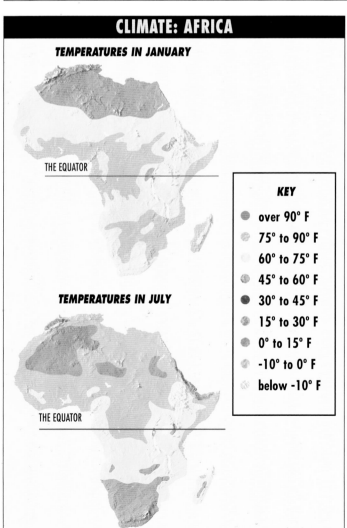

THE EQUATOR

TEMPERATURES IN JULY

THE EQUATOR

KEY
- over 90° F
- 75° to 90° F
- 60° to 75° F
- 45° to 60° F
- 30° to 45° F
- 15° to 30° F
- 0° to 15° F
- -10° to 0° F
- below -10° F

LAND USE

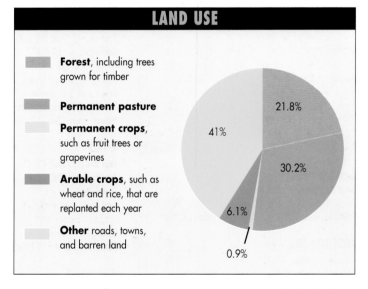

- **Forest**, including trees grown for timber
- **Permanent pasture**
- **Permanent crops**, such as fruit trees or grapevines
- **Arable crops**, such as wheat and rice, that are replanted each year
- **Other** roads, towns, and barren land

21.8%

41%

30.2%

6.1%

0.9%

THE AFRICAN BAOBAB TREE

The baobab tree grows in semi-arid places in sub-Saharan Africa.

- The tree can grow to 80 feet tall with a diameter around the trunk of over 30 feet. It is believed that baobabs can live for 1,000 years.

- Arabian legend says the devil plucked the baobab tree from the ground, then plunged it back in, upside down.

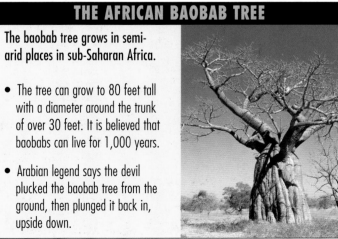

AFRICA FACTFILES

Each country-by-country factfile contains: **total area** of the country in square miles; **total population**; name of the **capital city**; the main **currency** used in the country; **main languages spoken** (listed in order of number of speakers); **top five farming products produced** (listed in order of importance to the country's economy); **natural resources** (of commercial importance); and a country's **status** if it is not independent.

ALGERIA
Total area (sq. miles): 919,595
Total population: 32,531,853
Capital city: Algiers
Currency: Algerian dinar (DZD)
Languages: Arabic, French, Berber dialects
Farming (top 5 products): Wheat, barley, oats, grapes, olives
Natural resources (top 5): Oil, natural gas, iron ore, phosphates, uranium

ANGOLA
Total area (sq. miles): 481,354
Total population: 11,190,786
Capital city: Luanda
Currency: Kwanza (AOA)
Languages: Portuguese, Bantu
Farming (top 5 products): Bananas, sugar cane, coffee, sisal, corn
Natural resources (top 5): Oil, diamonds, iron ore, phosphates, copper

BENIN
Total area (sq. miles): 43,483
Total population: 7,460,025
Capital city: Porto-Novo/Cotonou
Currency: Communaute Financiere Africaine franc (XOF)
Languages: French; Fon, Yoruba
Farming (top 5 products): Cotton, corn, cassava, yams, beans
Natural resources: Oil, limestone, marble, timber

BOTSWANA
Total area (sq. miles): 231,804
Total population: 1,640,115
Capital city: Gaborone
Currency: Pula (BWP)
Languages: Setswana, Kalanga
Farming (top 5 products): Livestock, sorghum, maize, millet, beans
Natural resources (top 5): Diamonds, copper, nickel, salt, coal

BURKINA FASO
Total area (sq. miles): 105,869
Total population: 13,925,313
Capital city: Ouagadougou
Currency: Communaute Financiere Africaine franc (XOF)
Languages: Moore, Jula, French
Farming (top 5 products): Cotton, peanuts, shea nuts, sesame, sorghum
Natural resources (top 5): Manganese, limestone, marble, gold, pumice

BURUNDI
Total area (sq. miles): 10,745
Total population: 6,370,609
Capital city: Bujumbura
Currency: Burundi franc (BIF)
Languages: Kirundi, French, Swahili
Farming (top 5 products): Coffee, cotton, tea, corn, sorghum
Natural resources (top 5): Nickel, uranium, peat, cobalt, copper

CAMEROON
Total area (sq. miles): 183,568
Total population: 16,380,005
Capital city: Yaounde
Currency: Communaute Financiere Africaine franc (XAF)
Languages: English, French, 24 African languages
Farming (top 5 products): Coffee, cocoa, cotton, rubber, bananas
Natural resources (top 5): Oil, bauxite, iron ore, timber, hydroelectric power

CAPE VERDE
Total area (sq. miles): 1,557
Total population: 418,224
Capital city: Praia
Currency: Cape Verdean escudo (CVE)
Languages: Portuguese; Crioulo
Farming (top 5 products): Bananas, corn, beans, sweet potatoes, sugar cane
Natural resources (top 5): Salt, basalt rock, limestone, kaolin, fish

CENTRAL AFRICAN REPUBLIC
Total area (sq. miles): 240,535
Total population: 3,799,897
Capital city: Bangui
Currency: Communaute Financiere Africaine franc (XAF)
Languages: French; Sangho
Farming (top 5 products): Cotton, coffee, tobacco, manioc, yams
Natural resources (top 5): Diamonds, uranium, timber, gold, oil

CHAD
Total area (sq. miles): 495,755
Total population: 9,826,419
Capital city: N'Djamena
Currency: Communaute Financiere Africaine franc (XAF)
Languages: French; Arabic, Sara, 120 different languages and dialects
Farming (top 5 products): Cotton, sorghum, millet, peanuts, rice
Natural resources (top 5): Oil, uranium, natron, kaolin, fish

COMOROS
Total area (sq. miles): 838
Total population: 671,247
Capital city: Moroni
Currency: Comoran franc (KMF)
Languages: Arabic, French, Shikomoro
Farming (top 5 products): Vanilla, cloves, perfume essences, copra, coconuts
Natural resources: Limited natural resources

CONGO (DEMOCRATIC REPUBLIC OF)
Total area (sq. miles): 905,568
Total population: 60,085,804
Capital city: Kinshasa
Currency: Congolese franc (CDF)
Languages: French, Lingala, Kingwana, Kikongo, Tshiluba
Farming (top 5 products): Coffee, sugar cane, palm oil, rubber, tea
Natural resources (top 5): Cobalt, copper, niobium, tantalum, oil

CONGO (REPUBLIC OF)
Total area (sq. miles): 132,047
Total population: 3,039,126
Capital city: Brazzaville
Currency: Communaute Financiere Africaine franc (XAF)
Languages: French, Lingala, Monokutuba
Farming (top 5 products): Cassava, sugar cane, rice, corn, peanuts
Natural resources (top 5): Oil, timber, potash, lead, zinc

COTE D'IVOIRE (IVORY COAST)
Total area (sq. miles): 124,503
Total population: 17,298,040
Capital city: Yamoussoukro/Abidjan
Currency: Communaute Financiere Africaine franc (XOF)
Languages: French, Dioula, and 60 indigenous dialects
Farming (top 5 products): Coffee, cocoa, bananas, palm kernels, corn
Natural resources (top 5): Oil, natural gas, diamonds, manganese, iron ore

DJIBOUTI
Total area (sq. miles): 8880
Total population: 476,703
Capital city: Djibouti
Currency: Bolivar (VEB)
Languages: French; Arabic, Somali, Afar
Farming: Fruits, vegetables, livestock (including camels)
Natural resources (top 5): Geothermal energy, gold; clay, granite, limestone

An elephant in the Ngorongoro Crater in Tanzania. The Crater is part of Africa's Great Rift Valley.

• See the GLOSSARY for words and terms used in these FACTFILES.

AFRICA Factfiles

EGYPT

Total area (sq. miles): 386,662
Total population: 77,505,756
Capital city: Cairo
Currency: Egyptian pound (EGP)
Languages: Arabic, English, French
Farming (top 5 products): Cotton, rice, corn, wheat, beans
Natural resources (top 5): Oil, natural gas, iron ore, phosphates, manganese

EQUATORIAL GUINEA
Total area (sq. miles): 10,831
Total population: 535,881
Capital city: Malabo
Currency: Communaute Financiere Africaine franc (XAF)
Languages: Spanish, French
Farming (top 5 products): Coffee, cocoa, rice, yams, cassava
Natural resources (top 5): Oil, natural gas, timber, gold, bauxite

ERITREA
Total area (sq. miles): 48,842
Total population: 4,561,599
Capital city: Asmara
Currency: Nafka (ERN)
Languages: Afar, Arabic, Tigre, Kuname, Tigrinya
Farming (top 5 products): Sorghum, lentils, vegetables, corn, cotton
Natural resources (top 5): Gold, potash, zinc, copper, salt

ETHIOPIA
Total area (sq. miles): 435,186
Total population: 75,053,286
Capital city: Addis Ababa
Currency: Birr (ETB)
Languages: Amharic, Tigrinya, Oromigna, Guaragigna, Somali, Arabic
Farming (top 5 products): Cereals, pulses, coffee, oilseed, sugar cane
Natural resources (top 5): Gold, platinum, copper, potash, natural gas

GABON
Total area (sq. miles): 103,347
Total population: 1,389,201
Capital city: Libreville
Currency: Communaute Financiere Africaine franc (XAF)
Languages: French, Fang, Myene, Nzebi
Farming (top 5 products): Cocoa, coffee, sugar cane, palm oil, rubber
Natural resources (top 5): Oil, natural gas, diamond, niobium, manganese

GAMBIA (THE)
Total area (sq. miles): 4,363
Total population: 1,593,256
Capital city: Banjul
Currency: Dalasi (GMD)
Languages: English, Mandinka, Wolof
Farming (top 5 products): Rice, millet, sorghum, peanuts, corn
Natural resources (top 5): Fish, titanium, tin, zircon, silica sand

GHANA
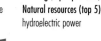
Total area (sq. miles): 92,456
Total population: 21,029,853
Capital city: Accra
Currency: Cedi (GHC)
Languages: Twi, Fante, Ga, Hausa, Dagbani, English
Farming (top 5 products): Cocoa, rice, coffee, cassava, peanuts
Natural resources (top 5): Gold, timber, industrial diamonds, bauxite, manganese

GUINEA
Total area (sq. miles): 94,926
Total population: 9,467,866
Capital city: Conakry
Currency: Guinean franc (GNF)
Languages: French
Farming (top 5 products): Rice, coffee, pineapples, palm kernels, cassava
Natural resources (top 5): Bauxite, iron ore, diamonds, gold, uranium

GUINEA-BISSAU

Total area (sq. miles): 13,946
Total population: 1,416,027
Capital city: Bissau
Currency: Communaute Financiere Africaine franc (XOF)
Languages: Crioulo, Balante, Pulaar, Mandjak, Mandinka, Portuguese
Farming (top 5 products): Rice, corn, beans, cassava, cashew nuts
Natural resources (top 5): Fish, timber, phosphates, bauxite, clay

KENYA

Total area (sq. miles): 224,962
Total population: 33,829,590
Capital city: Nairobi
Currency: Kenyan shilling (KES)
Languages: Swahili, English, Bantu
Farming (top 5 products): Tea, coffee, corn, wheat, sugar cane
Natural resources (top 5): Limestone, soda ash, salt, gemstones, fluorspar

LESOTHO
Total area (sq. miles): 11,720
Total population: 1,867,035
Capital city: Maseru
Currency: Loti (LSL), South African rand (ZAR)
Languages: Sesotho, English, Zulu, Xhosa
Farming (top 5 products): Corn, wheat, pulses, sorghum, barley
Natural resources: Diamonds, sand, clay, building stone

LIBERIA

Total area (sq. miles): 43,000
Total population: 3,482,211
Capital city: Monrovia
Currency: Liberian dollar (LRD)
Languages: Kpelle, English, Bassa
Farming (top 5 products): Rubber, coffee, cocoa, rice, cassava
Natural resources (top 5): Iron ore, timber, diamonds, gold, hydroelectric power

LIBYA
Total area (sq. miles): 679,362
Total population: 5,599,053
Capital city: Tripoli
Currency: Libyan dinar (LYD)
Languages: Arabic, Italian, English
Farming (top 5 products): Wheat, barley, olives, dates, citrus fruits
Natural resources: Oil, natural gas, gypsum

MADAGASCAR

Total area (sq. miles): 226,657
Total population: 18,040,341
Capital city: Antananarivo
Currency: Malagasy franc (MGF)
Languages: French, Malagasy
Farming (top 5 products): Coffee, vanilla, sugar cane, cloves, cocoa
Natural resources (top 5): Graphite, chromite, coal, bauxite, salt

MALAWI
Total area (sq. miles): 45,745
Total population: 12,158,924
Capital city: Lilongwe
Currency: Malawian Kwacha (MWK)
Languages: Chichewa, Chinyanja, Chiyao, Chitumbuka
Farming (top 5 products): Tobacco, sugar cane, cotton, tea, corn
Natural resources: Limestone, hydroelectric power

MALI
Total area (sq. miles): 478,767
Total population: 12,291,529
Capital city: Bamako
Currency: Communaute Financiere Africaine franc (XOF)
Languages: Bambara, Fulani, Songhai, French
Farming (top 5 products): Cotton, millet, rice, corn, vegetables
Natural resources (top 5): Gold, phosphates, kaolin, salt, limestone

MAURITANIA
Total area (sq. miles): 937,955
Total population: 3,086,859
Capital city: Nouakchott
Currency: Ouguiya (MRO)
Languages: Arabic, Pulaar, Soninke, French, Hassaniya, Wolof
Farming (top 5 products): Dates, millet, sorghum, rice, corn
Natural resources (top 5): Iron ore, gypsum, copper, phosphate, diamonds

MAURITIUS
Total area (sq. miles): 788
Total population: 1,230,602
Capital city: Port Louis
Currency: Mauritian rupee (MUR)
Languages: Creole, Bhojpuri, French
Farming (top 5 products): Sugar cane, tea, corn, potatoes, bananas
Natural resources: Fish

MAYOTTE
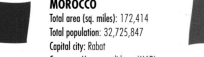
Total area (sq. miles): 144
Total population: 193,633
Capital city: Mamoutzou
Currency: Euro (EUR)
Languages: Mahorian, French
Farming: Vanilla, ylang-ylang (perfume essence), coffee, copra
Natural resources: Limited natural resources
Status: French overseas territory

MOROCCO
Total area (sq. miles): 172,414
Total population: 32,725,847
Capital city: Rabat
Currency: Moroccan dirham (MAD)
Languages: Arabic, Berber dialects, French
Farming (top 5 products): Barley, wheat, citrus fruits, grapes for wine, vegetables
Natural resources (top 5): Phosphates, iron ore, manganese, lead; zinc

• See the GLOSSARY for words and terms used in these FACTFILES.

MOZAMBIQUE

Total area (sq. miles): 309,496
Total population: 19,406,703
Capital city: Maputo
Currency: Metical (MZM)
Languages: Emakhuwa, Xichangana, Portuguese
Farming (top 5 products): Cotton, cashew nuts, sugar cane, tea, cassava
Natural resources (top 5): Coal, titanium, natural gas, hydroelectric power, tantalum

NAMIBIA

Total area (sq. miles): 318,696
Total population: 2,030,692
Capital city: Windhoek
Currency: Namibian dollar (NAD), South African rand (ZAR)
Languages: English, Afrikaans, German, indigenous languages
Farming: Millet, sorghum, peanuts, livestock
Natural resources (top 5): Diamonds, copper, uranium, gold, lead

NIGER

Total area (sq. miles): 489,191
Total population: 11,665,937
Capital city: Niamey
Currency: Communaute Financiere Africaine franc (XOF)
Languages: French, Hausa, Djerma
Farming (top 5 products): Peas (for cattle feed), cotton, peanuts, millet, sorghum
Natural resources (top 5): Uranium, coal, iron ore, tin, phosphates

NIGERIA

Total area (sq. miles): 356,669
Total population: 128,771,988
Capital city: Abuja
Currency: Naira (NGN)
Languages: Hausa, Yoruba, Igbo, English, Fulani
Farming (top 5 products): Cocoa, peanuts, palm oil, corn, rice
Natural resources (top 5): Natural gas, oil, tin, iron ore, coal

REUNION

Total area (sq. miles): 972
Total population: 776,948
Capital city: Saint-Denis
Currency: Euro (EUR)
Languages: French, Creole
Farming (top 5 products): Sugar cane, vanilla, tobacco, tropical fruits, vegetables
Natural resources (top 5): Fish, hydroelectric power
Status: French overseas territory

RWANDA

Total area (sq. miles): 10,169
Total population: 8,440,820
Capital city: Kigali
Currency: Rwandan franc (RWF)
Languages: Kinyarwanda, French, English, Kiswahili
Farming (top 5 products): Coffee, tea, pyrethrum, bananas, beans
Natural resources (top 5): Gold, tin ore, tungsten ore, methane; hydroelectric power

SAO TOME AND PRINCIPE

Total area (sq. miles): 386
Total population: 187,410
Capital city: Sao Tome
Currency: Dobra (STD)
Languages: Portuguese
Farming (top 5 products): Cocoa, coconuts, palm kernels, copra, cinnamon
Natural resources: Fish, hydroelectric power

SENEGAL

Total area (sq. miles): 75,749
Total population: 11,126,832
Capital city: Dakar
Currency: Communaute Financiere Africaine franc (XOF)
Languages: Wolof, French, Pulaar, Jola, Mandinka
Farming (top 5 products): Peanuts, millet, corn, sorghum, rice
Natural resources: Fish, phosphates, iron ore

SEYCHELLES

Total area (sq. miles): 176
Total population: 81,188
Capital city: Victoria
Currency: Seychelles rupee (SCR)
Languages: Creole, English
Farming (top 5 products): Coconuts, cinnamon, vanilla, sweet potatoes, cassava
Natural resources: Fish, copra, cinnamon trees

SIERRA LEONE

Total area (sq. miles): 27,699
Total population: 6,017,643
Capital city: Freetown
Currency: Leone (SLL)
Languages: Mende, Temne, Krio, English
Farming (top 5 products): Rice, coffee, cocoa, palm kernels, palm oil
Natural resources (top 5): Diamonds, titanium, bauxite, iron ore, gold

SOMALIA

Total area (sq. miles): 246,201
Total population: 8,591,629
Capital city: Mogadishu
Currency: Somali shilling (SOS)
Languages: Somali, Arabic, English
Farming (top 5 products): Livestock, bananas, sorghum, corn, coconuts
Natural resources: Uranium; unexploited resources, including iron ore, tin, gypsum, bauxite, and copper

SOUTH AFRICA

Total area (sq. miles): 471,000
Total population: 44,344,136
Capital city: Pretoria
Currency: Rand (ZAR)
Languages: IsiZulu, IsiXhosa, Afrikaans, Sepedi, English
Farming (top 5 products): Coffee, cotton, sugar cane, rice, potatoes
Natural resources (top 5): Gold, chromium, antimony, coal, iron ore

SUDAN

Total area (sq. miles): 967,499
Total population: 40,187,486
Capital city: Khartoum
Currency: Sudanese dinar (SDD)
Languages: Arabic, English
Farming (top 5 products): Cotton, groundnuts, sorghum, millet, wheat
Natural resources (top 5): Oil, small reserves of iron ore, copper, chromium ore, zinc, tungsten, mica, silver, and gold

SWAZILAND

Total area (sq. miles): 6,704
Total population: 1,173,900
Capital city: Mbabane/Lobamba
Currency: Lilangeni (SZL)
Languages: English, siSwati
Farming (top 5 products): Sugar cane, cotton, corn, tobacco, rice
Natural resources (top 5): Asbestos, coal, clay, cassiterite, hydroelectric power

TANZANIA

Total area (sq. miles): 364,900
Total population: 36,766,356
Capital city: Dar es Salaam/Dodoma
Currency: Tanzanian shilling (TZS)
Languages: Swahili, Kiunguja, English, Arabic
Farming (top 5 products): Coffee, sisal, tea, cotton, pyrethrum
Natural resources (top 5): Hydro-electric power, tin, phosphates, iron ore, coal

TOGO

Total area (sq. miles): 21,925
Total population: 5,681,519
Capital city: Lome
Currency: Communaute Financiere Africaine franc (XOF)
Languages: Mina, Ewe, Kabye, Dagomba, French
Farming (top 5 products): Coffee, cocoa, cotton, yams, cassava
Natural resources: Phosphates, limestone, marble

TUNISIA

Total area (sq. miles): 63,170
Total population: 10,074,951
Capital city: Tunis
Currency: Tunisian dinar (TND)
Languages: Arabic, French
Farming (top 5 products): Olives, olive oil, grain, dairy products, tomatoes
Natural resources (top 5): Oil, phosphates, iron ore, lead, zinc

UGANDA

Total area (sq. miles): 91,136
Total population: 27,269,482
Capital city: Kampala
Currency: Ugandan shilling (UGX)
Languages: Luganda, English, Swahili
Farming (top 5 products): Coffee, tea, cotton, tobacco, cassava
Natural resources (top 5): Copper, cobalt, hydroelectric power, limestone, salt

ZAMBIA

Total area (sq. miles): 290,586
Total population: 11,261,795
Capital city: Lusaka
Currency: Zambian kwacha (ZMK)
Languages: Bemba, Tonga, Nyanja, around 70 indigenous languages, English
Farming (top 5 products): Corn, sorghum, rice, peanuts, sunflower seeds
Natural resources (top 5): Copper, cobalt, zinc, lead, coal

ZIMBABWE

Total area (sq. miles): 150,804
Total population: 12,746,990
Capital city: Harare
Currency: Zimbabwean dollar (ZWD)
Languages: Shona, Ndebele, English
Farming (top 5 products): Corn, cotton, tobacco, wheat, coffee
Natural resources (top 5): Coal, chromium ore, asbestos, gold, nickel

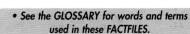

• See the GLOSSARY for words and terms used in these FACTFILES.

Eurasia is one giant landmass, comprising the continents of Europe and Asia. The vast Russian Federation's capital, Moscow, is in Europe, but the country spreads for thousands of miles across northern Asia. The landscapes of Europe vary from frozen regions in the Arctic Circle to hot countries that border the Mediterranean Sea. There are few remaining wilderness areas in Europe, and the continent is crossed by railways and roads joining large towns and cities.

The giant Rock of Gibraltar towers over the Strait of Gibraltar that links the Atlantic Ocean and the Mediterranean Sea. The rock is 1,398 feet high.

HIGHEST MOUNTAINS (BY COUNTRY)

NAME	LOCATION	HEIGHT (feet)
Elbrus	Russia	18,510*
Mont Blanc	France/Italy	15,774
Monte Rosa	Italy/Switzerland	15,203
Matterhorn	Italy	14,692

* Elbrus is the highest mountain in Europe.

LONGEST RIVERS

NAME	RIVER MOUTH	LENGTH (miles)
Volga	Caspian Sea	2,299
Danube	Black Sea	1,771
Ural	Caspian Sea	1,575
Dnieper	Black Sea	1,420

LARGEST ISLANDS

NAME		AREA (sq miles)
Great Britain (mainland)	North Sea/Altlantic Ocean	88,757
Iceland	Atlantic Ocean	39,769
Ireland	Atlantic Ocean	27,135

OIL CONSUMPTION

The amount of oil produced, bought and sold, and used in the world is measured in barrels. A barrel is equivalent to 42 gallons.

Russia is Europe's largest producer of oil—8,420,000 barrels per day

TOP 5 CONSUMERS OF OIL (USAGE PER DAY)

Germany	2,891,000 barrels
Russia	2,310,000 barrels
France	2,026,000 barrels
Italy	1,866,000 barrels
UK	1,692,000 barrels

FAST FACTS

• Vatican City is the smallest country in the world. It covers an area of just 109 acres in the centre of Rome. Vatican City is the headquarters of the Roman Catholic Church.

• Large parts of the Netherlands were once part of the North Sea. Long embankments, called *dykes*, have been built to hold back the ocean and parts of the coast have been reclaimed and pumped dry. These areas are called *polders*.

• The city of Venice, Italy is made up of 117 small islands of land that were built hundreds of years ago on salt marshes. The islands are joined to each other by 409 bridges. There are 150 seawater canals running between the islands. Workers, residents, and visitors travel around the city by boat.

• The coast of the United Kingdom has so many indents that no point in the UK is more than 70 miles from the sea.

POLITICAL MAP OF EUROPE

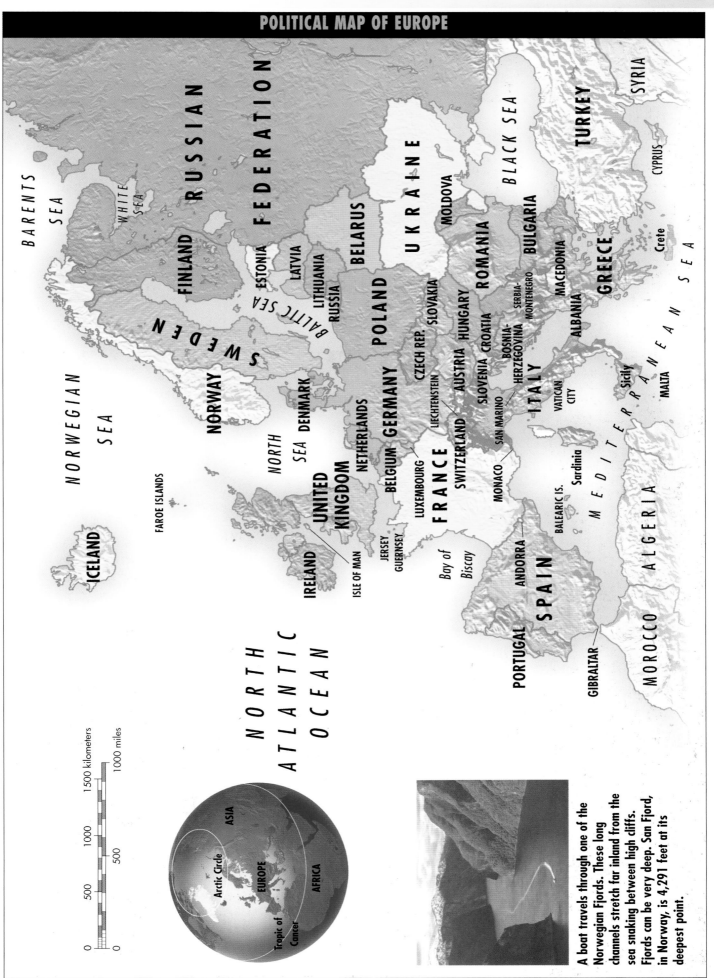

BARENTS SEA

WHITE SEA

RUSSIAN FEDERATION

FINLAND

NORWEGIAN SEA

SWEDEN

NORWAY

ESTONIA
LATVIA
LITHUANIA
RUSSIA
BALTIC SEA

BELARUS

UKRAINE

MOLDOVA

POLAND

ROMANIA

BULGARIA

BLACK SEA

TURKEY

SYRIA

CYPRUS

GREECE

MACEDONIA
SERBIA-MONTENEGRO
ALBANIA
Crete

CZECH REP.
SLOVAKIA
HUNGARY
SLOVENIA CROATIA
BOSNIA-HERZEGOVINA

AUSTRIA

LIECHTENSTEIN

SWITZERLAND

SAN MARINO

ITALY
VATICAN CITY

MEDITERRANEAN SEA

MALTA

Sicily

Sardinia

BALEARIC IS.

NORTH SEA
DENMARK

NETHERLANDS

BELGIUM GERMANY

LUXEMBOURG

FRANCE

MONACO

UNITED KINGDOM

IRELAND

ISLE OF MAN

JERSEY
GUERNSEY

Bay of Biscay

ANDORRA

SPAIN

PORTUGAL

GIBRALTAR

MOROCCO

ALGERIA

FAROE ISLANDS

ICELAND

NORTH ATLANTIC OCEAN

1500 kilometers
1000 miles
1000
500
500
0
0

ASIA

Arctic Circle

EUROPE

AFRICA

Tropic of Cancer

A boat travels through one of the Norwegian Fjords. These long channels stretch far inland from the sea snaking between high cliffs. Fjords can be very deep. San Fjord, in Norway, is 4,291 feet at its deepest point.

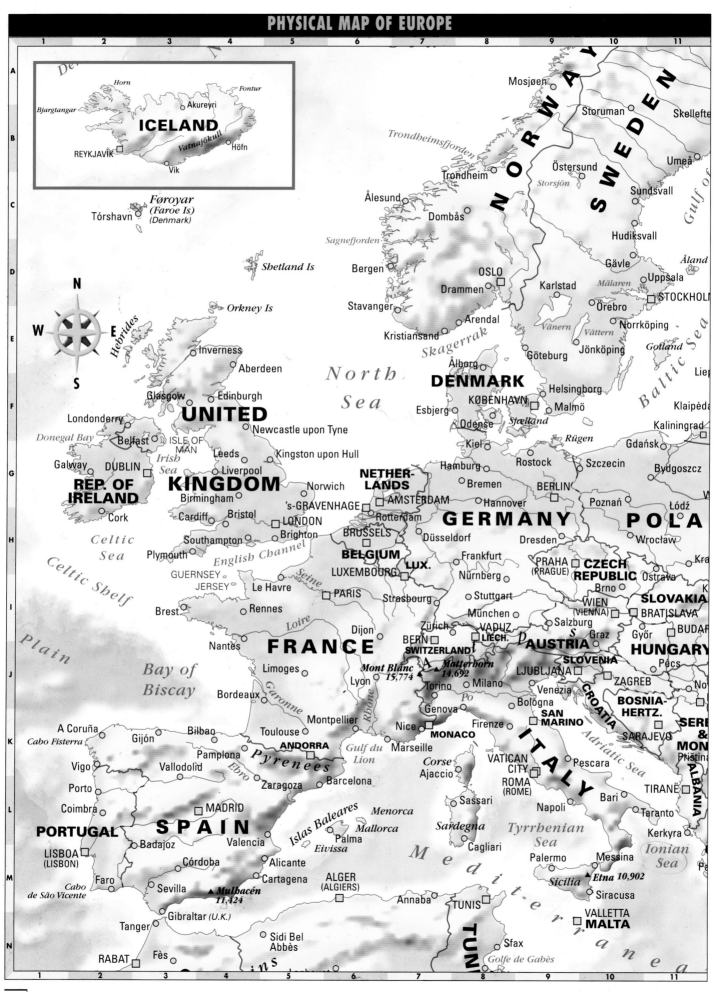

PHYSICAL MAP OF EUROPE

| | 12 | 13 | 14 | 15 | 16 | 17 | 18 | 19 | 20 | 21 | 22 |

Miller Cylindrical Projection

□ Capital city
□ Administrative capital
○ Other city or town
▲ Mountain summit (heights in feet)
Dry salt lake
Marsh
— International boundary
.... International boundary, disputed
- - - Administrative boundary

Land heights Feet	Sea depths Feet
26,200	1,600
23,000	3,300
19,700	6,600
16,400	13,100
13,100	16,400
9,800	19,700
6,600	23,200
3,300	
1,600	
700	
0	
Land below sea level	

Gällivare
Boden
Kemi
Rovaniemi

FINLAND

Oulu
Ozero Topozero
White Sea

Kajaani
Oulujärvi

Lieksa
Ozero Vygozero

Vaasa
Kuopio
Orivesi

Pori
Jyväskylä
Petrozavodsk
Onezh. Ozero

Tampere
Saimaa
Ladozhskoye Ozero
Ozero Beloye

Turku
HELSINKI
Gulf of Finland
Vyborg
Sankt-Peterburg
Vologda

TALLINN
Kingisepp
Cherepovets
Rybinskoye Vodokhranilishche

ESTONIA
Tartu
Lake Piepus
Velikiy Novgorod
Kostroma

RUSSIAN

Kotel'nich
Kirov

Ventspils
Valmiera
Ozero Il'men'
Pskov
Yaroslavl'
Ivanovo
Nizhniy-Novgorod
Izhevsk

FEDERATION

āja
RĪGA
LATVIA
Rēzekne
Velikiye Luki
Tver'
Vladimir
Murom
Arzamas
Kazan'
Naberez. Chelny

Šiauliai
Daugavpils

LITHUANIA
VILNIUS
Vitsyebsk
Smolensk
MOSKVA (MOSCOW)
Kaluga
Tula
Ryazan'
Ul'yanovsk
Dimitrovgrad

RUS. FED.
Kaunas
MINSK
Mahilyow
Volga

Hrodna
Bryansk
Orel
Lipetsk
Penza
Syzran'
Samara

Białystok

BELARUS
Klintsy
Tambov

WARSZAWA
Brest
Homyel'
Chernihiv
Kursk
Voronezh
Saratov
Balakovo
Ural'sk

ND
Lublin
Korosten'
Rivne
KYIV (KIEV)
Sumy
Belgorod
Kamyshin
Ura

ców
L'viv
Zhytomyr

UKRAINE
Poltava
Kharkiv
Volgograd

ošice
Uzhorod
Vinnytsya
Cherkasy
Dnipropetrovs'k
Luhans'k
Akhtubinsk
K

Carpathian Mts
MOLDOVA
Kryvyy Rih
Zaporizhzhya
Donets'k
Volgodonsk
Atyrau

Oradea
Iaşi
CHIŞINĂU
Mykolaviv
Mariupol
Rostov-na-Donu
Astrakhan'
Volga

Arad
Cluj-Napoca
Odesa
Sea of Azov
Elista

ROMANIA
Braşov
Krasnodar
Stavropol'

vi Sad
BEOGRAD (BELGRADE)
BUCUREŞTI (BUCHAREST)
Sevastopol'
Kerch
Maykop
Nevinnomyssk

BIA
Craiova
Sudak
Elbrus 18,510
Nal'chik
Aktau

Niš
Constanţa
Danube
Black Sea
Sokhumi
Grozny
Caspian Sea

TE.
BULGARIA
Varna
K'ut'aisi
Caucasus
Makhachkala

SOFIYA
Burgas
Sinop
GEORGIA

SKOPJE
Edirne
İstanbul
Zonguldak
Samsun
Bat'umi
T'BILISI
Zaliv Kara Gol

MAC.
Thessaloniki
Bursa
Sakarya
Çorum
Trabzon
Gyumri
Gänca
BAKI

Larisa
İzmir
ANKARA
Sivas
Erzurum
YEREVAN
ARMENIA
AZERBAIJAN
Turkm

GREECE
TURKEY
Ararat 16,946
AZER.
Xankändi
Äli Bayramli

ATHINA (ATHENS)
Isparta
Konya
Kahramanmaraş
Lake Van
Van
Tabrīz
Ardabīl
Nebitdag

Tripoli
Antalya
Adana
Al Hasakah
Orūmīyeh
Damāvand 18,386

Chania
Dodekanisos
Ródos
Rodos
Adana
Halab
Ar Raqqah
Tigris
TEHRĀN
Elburz

Kriti (Crete)
Iraklion
LEFKOŞIA (NICOSIA)
Al Lādhiqīyah
Tartus
Hamāh
Qom
Das.

CYPRUS
LEBANON
Himş
Euphrates
Kermānshāh

DIMASHQ
SYRIA

EUROPE

HABITATS

This map shows the different types of habitats across the continent.

KEY
- Ice and snow
- Tundra
- Mountains/barren land
- Forest
- Grassland
- Semidesert
- Desert

THE EUROPEAN UNION

The European Union (EU) is an organization set up to allow European countries to support each other.

WHAT DOES THE EU DO?
The EU has set up laws that help member countries trade easily, allow EU workers to work in any other EU country without permits or visas, and protect EU workers.

THE EEC
The organization began in 1957. Six European countries formed the European Economic Community (EEC) with the aim of abolishing tariffs and trading restrictions between members. The countries were Belgium, France, Germany, Italy, Luxembourg, and the Netherlands.

THE EU
More European countries joined the group and in 1992, the organization became the EU. Member states agreed to work together in many areas including defence, foreign policy, and social policies.

Today, 25 European countries are members of the European Union.

EUROPEAN UNION MEMBERS

The 25 EU member states and the year they joined the Union:

Belgium	1957	Greece	1981	Poland	2004
France	1957	Spain	1986	Czech Republic	2004
Germany	1957	Portugal	1986	Slovakia	2004
Italy	1957	Austria	1995	Hungary	2004
Luxembourg	1957	Finland	1995	Slovenia	2004
The Netherlands	1957	Sweden	1995	Malta	2004
Denmark	1973	Estonia	2004	Cyprus	2004
Ireland	1973	Latvia	2004		
United Kingdom	1973	Lithuania	2004		

EU FLAG AND THE EURO

The European Union flag has 12 stars for the 12 countries that were members when the EU was named in 1992.

- EU member countries have an EU FLAG in the EUROPE FACTFILES which begin on page 41.

Total population of 25 EU member states:

457,000,000

Total area of EU zone:

1,535,286 square miles

The Euro was launched as a unit of exchange throughout the European Union on January 1, 1999.

The euro is used as currency by 12 EU countries: Austria, Belgium, Finland, France, Germany, Greece, Ireland, Italy, Luxembourg, Netherlands, Portugal, and Spain.

LAND USE

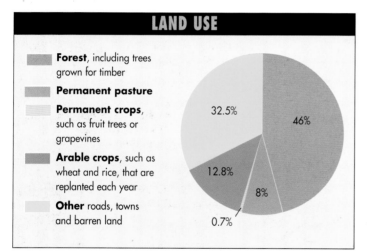

- **Forest**, including trees grown for timber
- **Permanent pasture**
- **Permanent crops**, such as fruit trees or grapevines
- **Arable crops**, such as wheat and rice, that are replanted each year
- **Other** roads, towns and barren land

46%
32.5%
12.8%
8%
0.7%

CLIMATE: EUROPE

KEY
- over 90° F
- 75° to 90° F
- 60° to 75° F
- 45° to 60° F
- 30° to 45° F
- 15° to 30° F
- 0° to 15° F
- -10° to 0° F
- below -10° F

TEMPERATURES IN JANUARY

ARCTIC CIRCLE

TEMPERATURES IN JULY

ARCTIC CIRCLE

EUROPE FACTFILES

Each country-by-country factfile contains: **total area** of the country in square miles; **total population**; name of the **capital city**; the main **currency** used in the country; **main languages spoken** (listed in order of number of speakers); **top five farming products produced** (listed in order of importance to the country's economy); **natural resources** (of commercial importance); and a country's **status** if it is not independent.

ALBANIA
Total area (sq. miles): 11,100
Total population: 3,563,112
Capital city: Tirana
Currency: Lek (ALL)
Languages: Albanian, Greek, Vlach
Farming (top 5 products): Wheat, corn, potatoes, vegetables, fruit
Natural resources (top 5): Oil, natural gas, coal, bauxite, chromite

ANDORRA
Total area (sq. miles): 181
Total population: 70,549
Capital city: Andorra la Vella
Currency: Euro (EUR)
Languages: Catalan, French, Castilian, Portuguese
Farming (top 5 products): Rye, wheat, barley, oats, vegetables
Natural resources (top 5): Hydroelectric power, mineral water, timber, iron ore, lead

AUSTRIA
Total area (sq. miles): 32,382
Total population: 8,184,691
Capital city: Vienna
Currency: Euro (EUR)
Languages: German, Slovene, Croatian, Hungarian
Farming (top 5 products): Cereal crops, potatoes, sugar beets, grapes for wine, fruit
Natural resources (top 5): Oil, coal, lignite, timber, iron ore

BELARUS
Total area (sq. miles): 80,155
Total population: 10,300,483
Capital city: Minsk
Currency: Belarusian ruble (BYB/BYR)
Languages: Belarusian, Russian
Farming (top 5 products): Cereal crops, potatoes, vegetables, sugar beets, flax
Natural resources (top 5): Timber; peat; small quantities oil and natural gas; granite; limestone

BELGIUM
Total area (sq. miles): 11,787
Total population: 10,364,388
Capital city: Brussels
Currency: Euro (EUR)
Languages: Dutch, French, German
Farming (top 5 products): Sugar beets, vegetables, fruits, cereal crops, tobacco
Natural resources: Construction materials, silica sand, carbonates

BOSNIA–HERZEGOVINA
Total area (sq miles): 19,741
Total population: 4,025,476
Capital city: Sarajevo
Currency: Marka (BAM)
Languages: Bosnian; Croatian; Serbian
Farming (top 5 products): Wheat; corn; fruits; vegetables; livestock
Natural resources (top 5): Coal; iron ore; bauxite; copper; lead

BULGARIA
Total area (sq. miles): 42,823
Total population: 7,450,349
Capital city: Sofia
Currency: Lev (BGL)
Languages: Bulgarian, Turkish, Roma
Farming (top 5 products): Vegetables, fruits, tobacco, livestock, grapes for wine
Natural resources (top 5): Bauxite, copper, lead, zinc, coal

CROATIA
Total area (sq. miles): 21,831
Total population: 4,495,904
Capital city: Zagreb
Currency: Kuna (HRK)
Languages: Croatian, Serbian
Farming (top 5 products): Wheat, corn, sugar beets, sunflower seeds, barley
Natural resources (top 5): Oil, coal, bauxite, iron ore, calcium

CYPRUS
Total area (sq. miles): 3,571
Total population: 780,133
Capital city: Nicosia
Currency: Cypriot pound (CYP); Turkish lira (TRL)
Languages: Greek, Turkish, English
Farming (top 5 products): Citrus fruits, vegetables, barley, grapes, olives
Natural resources (top 5): Copper, pyrites, asbestos, gypsum, timber

CZECH REPUBLIC
Total area (sq. miles): 30,450
Total population: 10,241,138
Capital city: Prague
Currency: Czech koruna (CZK)
Languages: Czech
Farming (top 5 products): Wheat, potatoes, sugar beets, hops, fruit
Natural resources (top 5): Coal, kaolin, clay, graphite, timber

DENMARK
Total area (sq miles): 16,639
Total population: 5,432,335
Capital city: Copenhagen
Currency: Danish krone (DKK)
Languages: Danish; Faroese; Greenlandic; German
Farming (top 5 products): Barley; wheat; potatoes; sugar beets; pigs
Natural resources (top 5): Oil; natural gas; fish; salt; limestone

ESTONIA
Total area (sq. miles): 17,462
Total population: 1,332,893
Capital city: Tallinn
Currency: Estonian kroon (EEK)
Languages: Estonian, Russian
Farming: Potatoes, vegetables, livestock, dairy products
Natural resources (top 5): Oil shale, peat, phosphorite, clay, limestone

FAROE ISLANDS
Total area (sq. miles): 540
Total population: 49,962
Capital city: Caracas
Currency: Danish krone (DKK)
Languages: Faroese, Danish
Farming (top 5 products): Milk, potatoes, vegetables, sheep, salmon
Natural resources: Fish, whales, hydroelectric power
Status: Self-governing Danish territory

FINLAND
Total area (sq. miles): 130,559
Total population: 5,223,442
Capital city: Helsinki
Currency: Euro (EUR)
Languages: Finnish, Swedish
Farming (top 5 products): Barley, wheat, sugar beets, potatoes, cattle
Natural resources (top 5): Timber, iron ore, copper, lead, zinc

FRANCE
Total area (sq. miles): 211,209
Total population: 60,656,178
Capital city: Paris
Currency: Euro (EUR)
Languages: French
Farming (top 5 products): Wheat, cereal crops, sugar beets, potatoes, grapes for wine
Natural resources (top 5): Coal, iron ore, bauxite, zinc, uranium

• See the GLOSSARY for words and terms used in these FACTFILES.

EUROPE Factfiles

GERMANY

Total area (sq. miles): 137,847
Total population: 82,431,390
Capital city: Berlin
Currency: Euro (EUR)
Languages: German
Farming (top 5 products): Potatoes, wheat, barley, sugar beets, fruit
Natural resources (top 5): Coal, lignite, natural gas, iron ore, copper

GIBRALTAR
Total area (sq. miles): 2.5
Total population: 27,884
Capital city: Gibraltar
Currency: Gibraltar pound (GIP)
Languages: English, Spanish, Italian, Portuguese
Farming: No farming
Natural resources: No natural resources
Status: United Kingdom overseas territory

GREECE
Total area (sq. miles): 50,942
Total population: 10,668,354
Capital city: Athens
Currency: Euro (EUR)
Languages: Greek
Farming (top 5 products): Wheat, corn, barley, sugar beets, olives
Natural resources (top 5): Lignite, oil, iron ore, bauxite, lead

GUERNSEY
Total area (sq. miles): 30
Total population: 65,228
Capital city: Saint Peter Port
Currency: British pound (GBP)
Languages: English, French
Farming (top 5 products): Tomatoes, cut flowers, sweet peppers, aubergines, fruit
Natural resources: Arable land
Status: United Kingdom Crown Dependency

HUNGARY

Total area (sq. miles): 35,919
Total population: 10,006,835
Capital city: Budapest
Currency: Forint (HUF)
Languages: Hungarian
Farming (top 5 products): Wheat, corn, sunflower seeds, potatoes, sugar beets
Natural resources: Bauxite, coal, natural gas

ICELAND
Total area (sq. miles): 39,769
Total population: 296,737
Capital city: Reykjavik
Currency: Icelandic krona (ISK)
Languages: Icelandic, English
Farming: Potatoes, vegetables, sheep, dairy products
Natural resources: Fish, hydroelectric power, geothermal power

IRELAND

Total area (sq. miles): 27,135
Total population: 4,015,676
Capital city: Dublin
Currency: Euro (EUR)
Languages: English, Irish (Gaelic/Gaeilge)
Farming (top 5 products): Turnips, barley, potatoes, sugar beets, wheat
Natural resources (top 5): Natural gas, peat, copper, lead, zinc

ISLE OF MAN
Total area (sq. miles): 221
Total population: 75,049
Capital city: Douglas
Currency: British pound (GBP)
Languages: English, Manx Gaelic
Farming: Cereal crops, vegetables, livestock, poultry
Natural resources: No natural resources
Status: United Kingdom Crown Dependency

ITALY

Total area (sq. miles): 116,306
Total population: 58,103,033
Capital city: Rome
Currency: Euro (EUR)
Languages: Italian
Farming (top 5 products): Fruit, vegetables, grapes for wine, potatoes, sugar beets
Natural resources (top 5): Coal, mercury, zinc, potash, marble

JERSEY
Total area (sq. miles): 45
Total population: 90,812
Capital city: Saint Helier
Currency: British pound (GBP)
Languages: English
Farming (top 5 products): Potatoes, cauliflower, tomatoes, cattle, dairy products
Natural resources: Arable land
Status: United Kingdom Crown Dependency

LATVIA
Total area (sq. miles): 24,938
Total population: 2,290,237
Capital city: Riga
Currency: Latvian lat (LVL)
Languages: Latvian, Russian
Farming (top 5 products): Cereal crops, sugar beets, potatoes, vegetables, livestock
Natural resources (top 5): Peat, limestone, dolomite, amber, hydroelectric power

LIECHTENSTEIN
Total area (sq. miles): 62
Total population: 33,717
Capital city: Vaduz
Currency: Swiss franc (CHF)
Languages: German
Farming (top 5 products): Wheat, barley, corn, potatoes, livestock
Natural resources: hydroelectric power potential, arable land

LITHUANIA

Total area (sq. miles): 25,174
Total population: 3,596,617
Capital city: Vilnius
Currency: Litas (LTL)
Languages: Lithuanian, Russian
Farming (top 5 products): Cereal crops, potatoes, sugar beets, flax, vegetables
Natural resources: Peat, arable land

LUXEMBOURG
Total area (sq. miles): 998
Total population: 468,571
Capital city: Luxembourg
Currency: Euro (EUR)
Languages: Luxembourgish, German, French
Farming (top 5 products): Barley, oats, potatoes, wheat, fruit
Natural resources: Arable land

MACEDONIA
Total area (sq. miles): 9781
Total population: 2,045,262
Capital city: Skopje
Currency: Macedonian denar (MKD)
Languages: Macedonian, Albanian
Farming (top 5 products): Wheat, grapes, rice, tobacco, corn
Natural resources (top 5): Iron ore, copper, lead, zinc, chromite

MALTA

Total area (sq. miles): 122
Total population: 398,534
Capital city: Valletta
Currency: Maltese lira (MTL)
Languages: Maltese, English
Farming (top 5 products): Potatoes, cauliflowers, grapes, wheat, barley
Natural resources: Limestone, salt, arable land

MOLDOVA
Total area (sq. miles): 13,067
Total population: 4,455,421
Capital city: Chisinau
Currency: Moldovan leu (MDL)
Languages: Moldovan, Russian, Gagauz (a Turkish dialect)
Farming (top 5 products): Vegetables, fruit, grapes for wine, cereal crops, sugar beets
Natural resources: Lignite, phosphorites, gypsum

MONACO
Total area (sq. miles): 0.75
Total population: 32,409
Capital city: Monaco
Currency: Euro (EUR)
Languages: French, English, Italian, Monegasque
Farming: No farming
Natural resources: No natural resources

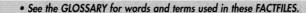
• See the GLOSSARY for words and terms used in these FACTFILES.

NETHERLANDS

Total area (sq. miles): 16,033
Total population: 16,407,491
Capital city: Amsterdam
Currency: Euro (EUR)
Languages: Dutch; Frisian
Farming (top 5 products): Cereal crops, potatoes, sugar beets, fruit, vegetables
Natural resources (top 5): Natural gas, oil, peat, limestone, salt

NORWAY

Total area (sq. miles): 125,182
Total population: 4,593,041
Capital city: Oslo
Currency: Norwegian krone (NOK)
Languages: Bokmal Norwegian, Nynorsk Norwegian, small Sami and Finnish-speaking minorities
Farming (top 5 products): Barley, wheat, potatoes, livestock, milk
Natural resources (top 5): Oil, natural gas, iron ore, copper, lead

POLAND

Total area (sq. miles): 120,728
Total population: 38,635,144
Capital city: Warsaw
Currency: Zloty (PLN)
Languages: Polish
Farming (top 5 products): Potatoes, fruit, vegetables, wheat, poultry
Natural resources (top 5): Coal, sulphur, copper, natural gas, silver

PORTUGAL

Total area (sq. miles): 35,672
Total population: 10,566,212
Capital city: Lisbon
Currency: Euro (EUR)
Languages: Portuguese, Mirandese
Farming (top 5 products): Cereal crops, potatoes, olives, grapes, livestock
Natural resources (top 5): Fish, cork forests, iron ore, copper, zinc

ROMANIA

Total area (sq. miles): 91,699
Total population: 22,329,977
Capital city: Bucharest
Currency: Leu (ROL)
Languages: Romanian, Hungarian, German
Farming (top 5 products): Wheat, corn, barley, sugar beets, sunflower seeds
Natural resources (top 5): Oil, timber, natural gas, coa, iron ore

RUSSIAN FEDERATION

Total area (sq. miles): 6,592,772
Total population: 143,420,309
Capital city: Moscow
Currency: Russian ruble (RUR)
Languages: Russian
Farming (top 5 products): Cereal crops, sugar beets, sunflower seeds, vegetables, fruit
Natural resources (top 5): Oil, natural gas, coal, many minerals, timber

SAN MARINO

Total area (sq. miles): 24
Total population: 28,880
Capital city: San Marino
Currency: Euro (EUR)
Languages: Italian
Farming (top 5 products): Wheat, grapes, corn, olives, livestock
Natural resources: Stone for construction

SERBIA MONTENEGRO

Total area (sq. miles): 39,518
Total population: 10,829,175
Capital city: Belgrade
Currency: Yugoslav dinar (YUM), Euro (EUR)
Languages: Serbian, Albanian
Farming (top 5 products): Coffee, cotton, sugar cane, rice, potatoes
Natural resources (top 5): Oil, gas, coal, iron ore, bauxite

SLOVAKIA

Total area (sq. miles): 18,859
Total population: 5,431,363
Capital city: Bratislava
Currency: Slovak koruna (SKK)
Languages: Slovak; Hungarian
Farming (top 5 products): Cereal crops, potatoes, sugar beets, hops, fruit
Natural resources (top 5): Coal, lignite, iron ore, copper, manganese

SLOVENIA

Total area (sq. miles): 7827
Total population: 2,011,070
Capital city: Ljubljana
Currency: Tolar (SIT)
Languages: Slovenian, Serbo-Croatian
Farming (top 5 products): Potatoes, hops, wheat, sugar beets, corn
Natural resources (top 5): Lignite, lead, zinc, mercury, uranium

SPAIN

Total area (sq. miles): 194,897
Total population: 40,341,462
Capital city: Madrid
Currency: Euro (EUR)
Languages: Castilian Spanish, Catalan, Galician, Basque
Farming (top 5 products): Cereal crops, vegetables, olives, grapes for wine, sugar beets
Natural resources (top 5): Coal, lignite, iron ore, copper, lead

SWEDEN

Total area (sq. miles): 173,732
Total population: 9,001,774
Capital city: Stockholm
Currency: Swedish krona (SEK)
Languages: Swedish, small Sami and Finnish-speaking minorities
Farming (top 5 products): Barley, wheat, sugar beets, livestock, milk
Natural resources (top 5): Iron ore, copper, lead, zinc, gold

SWITZERLAND

Total area (sq. miles): 15,942
Total population: 7,489,370
Capital city: Bern
Currency: Swiss franc (CHF)
Languages: German; French, Italian
Farming (top 5 products): Cereal crops, fruit, vegetables, livestock, eggs
Natural resources: Hydroelectric power potential, timber, salt

TURKEY

Total area (sq. miles): 301,384
Total population: 69,660,559
Capital city: Ankara
Currency: New Turkish lira (YTL)
Languages: Turkish, Kurdish, Arabic, Armenian, Greek
Farming (top 5 products): Tobacco, cotton, cereals, olives, sugar beets
Natural resources (top 5): Coal, iron ore, copper, chromium, antimony

UKRAINE

Total area (sq. miles): 233,090
Total population: 47,425,336
Capital city: Kiev
Currency: Hryvnia (UAH)
Languages: Ukrainian, Russian
Farming (top 5 products): Cereal crops, sugar beets, sunflower seeds, vegetables, cattle
Natural resources (top 5): Iron ore, coal, manganese, natural gas, oil

UNITED KINGDOM

Total area (sq. miles): 94,526
Total population: 60,441,457
Capital city: London
Currency: British pound (GBP)
Languages: English
Farming (top 5 products): Cereal crops, oilseed, potatoes, vegetables, livestock
Natural resources (top 5): Coal, oil, natural gas, iron ore, lead

VATICAN CITY

Total area (sq. miles): 0.17
Total population: 921
Capital city: Vatican City
Currency: Euro (EUR)
Languages: Italian, Latin
Farming: No farming
Natural resources: No natural resources

The Alps mountain range stretches from France, through Switzerland, Liechtenstein, and Italy, to Austria and Slovenia. The range is 750 miles long with a width of 125 miles at its widest sections.

• See the GLOSSARY for words and terms used in these FACTFILES.

Asia is the world's largest continent, and it includes many vast countries with huge populations, such as China, India, and the Russian Federation. The landscape includes Arctic tundra, tropical rainforests, and the world's highest mountains, the Himalayas. Rice is Asia's most important food crop, and paddy fields can be seen dotted across Southeast Asia—one fifth of the world's rice is grown in this part of Asia.

A worldwide symbol of conservation, China's Giant Panda lives in the mountainous forests of southwestern China.

HIGHEST MOUNTAINS (BY COUNTRY)

• See page 10 WORLD'S 10 HIGHEST MOUNTAINS for information on Asia's highest mountains.

NAME	LOCATION	HEIGHT (feet)
Qullai Ismoili Somoni	Tajikistan	24,590
Damavand	Iran	18,386
Punkak Jaya	Indonesia	16,503
Kinabalu	Borneo, Malaysia	13,432
Fuji San	Japan	12,388

LARGEST LAKES

NAME	LOCATION	AREA (sq. miles)
Caspian Sea	Asia	143,244*
Aral Sea	Kazakhstan/Uzbekistan	11,076
Lake Balqash	Kazakhstan	7,143
Ysyk Kol	Kyrgyzstan	2,394

* The Caspian Sea is the world's largest lake.

LARGEST ISLANDS

NAME	LOCATION	AREA (sq miles)
Borneo	Southeast Asia	287,399
Sumatra	Indonesia	182,858
Honshu	Japan	87,992

• See page 10 WORLD'S 10 LONGEST RIVERS

OIL CONSUMPTION

The amount of oil produced, bought and sold, and used in the world is measured in barrels. A barrel is equivalent to 42 gallons.

Saudi Arabia is the world's largest producer of oil— 9,021,000 barrels each day.

25% of the world's proven oil reserves are in Saudi Arabia.

TOP 5 CONSUMERS OF OIL IN ASIA (USAGE PER DAY)

Japan	5,290,000 barrels
China	4,956,000 barrels
India	2,130,000 barrels
South Korea	2,070,000 barrels
Saudi Arabia	1,550,000 barrels

SIBERIA

The Russian Federation covers around 11% of the Earth's surface.

• Over 5 million square miles of the country form the great barren plains, tundra regions and taiga forests of Siberia.

• The Trans-Siberian railway is the longest stretch of railway track in the world. The 5,778-mile journey from Moscow to Vladivostok (on the Pacific coast) takes around eight days.

POLITICAL MAP OF ASIA

Kuwait is a desert country with no rivers or lakes. Sea water is processed for drinking and stored in huge water towers.

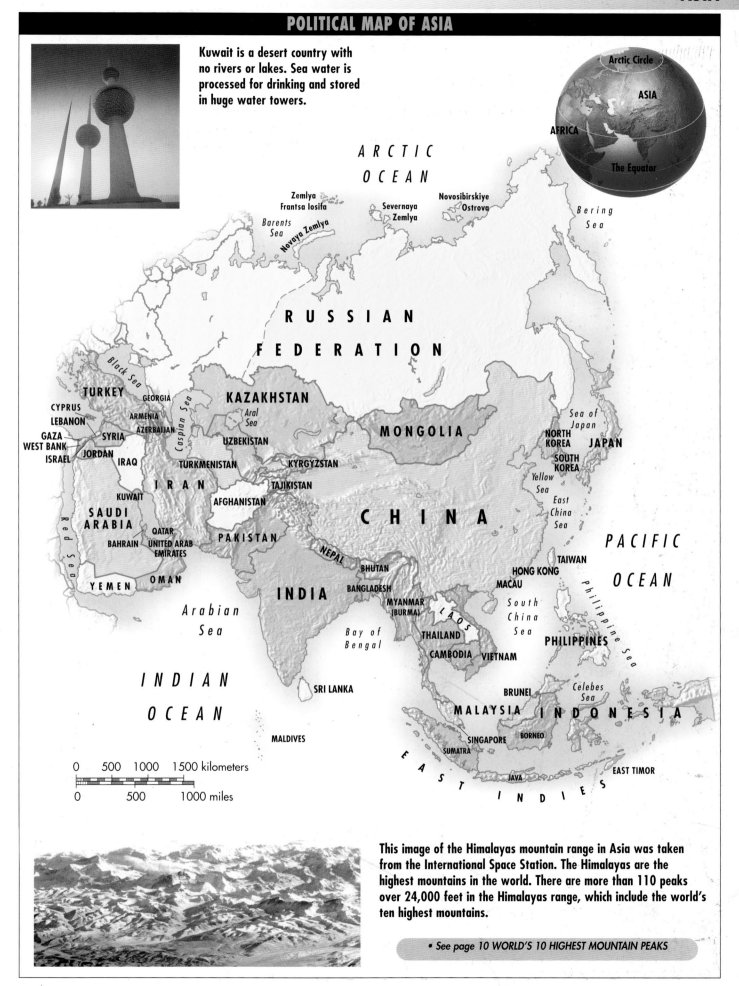

Arctic Circle

ASIA

AFRICA

The Equator

ARCTIC OCEAN

Zemlya Frantsa Iosifa

Novaya Zemlya

Barents Sea

Severnaya Zemlya

Novosibirskiye Ostrova

Bering Sea

RUSSIAN FEDERATION

Black Sea

TURKEY

GEORGIA

CYPRUS

LEBANON

GAZA

WEST BANK

ISRAEL

SYRIA

JORDAN

ARMENIA

AZERBAIJAN

Caspian Sea

IRAQ

IRAN

KUWAIT

SAUDI ARABIA

QATAR

BAHRAIN

UNITED ARAB EMIRATES

YEMEN

OMAN

Red Sea

KAZAKHSTAN

Aral Sea

UZBEKISTAN

TURKMENISTAN

KYRGYZSTAN

TAJIKISTAN

AFGHANISTAN

PAKISTAN

MONGOLIA

CHINA

NEPAL

BHUTAN

INDIA

BANGLADESH

MYANMAR (BURMA)

Arabian Sea

Bay of Bengal

THAILAND

LAOS

CAMBODIA

VIETNAM

NORTH KOREA

SOUTH KOREA

Sea of Japan

JAPAN

Yellow Sea

East China Sea

HONG KONG

MACAU

TAIWAN

South China Sea

PACIFIC OCEAN

Philippine Sea

PHILIPPINES

INDIAN OCEAN

MALDIVES

SRI LANKA

BRUNEI

Celebes Sea

MALAYSIA

INDONESIA

SINGAPORE

BORNEO

SUMATRA

JAVA

EAST TIMOR

EAST INDIES

0   500   1000   1500 kilometers

0   500   1000 miles

This image of the Himalayas mountain range in Asia was taken from the International Space Station. The Himalayas are the highest mountains in the world. There are more than 110 peaks over 24,000 feet in the Himalayas range, which include the world's ten highest mountains.

• See page 10 WORLD'S 10 HIGHEST MOUNTAIN PEAKS

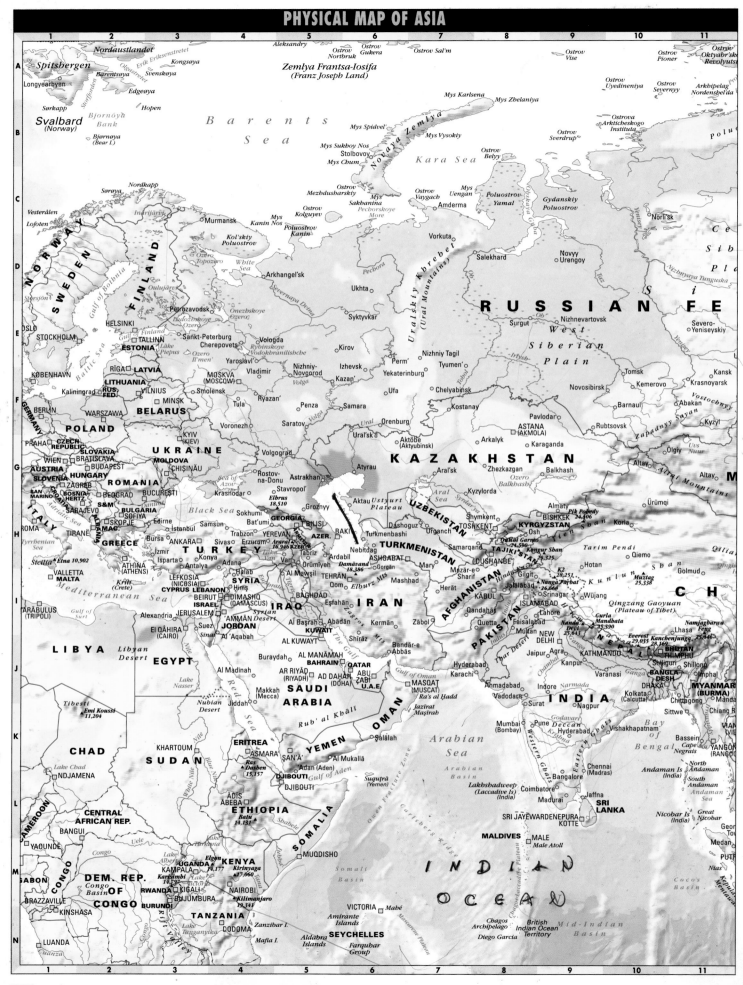

Spitsbergen
Nordaustlandet
Kongsøya
Erik Eriksenstretet
Svenskøya
Edgeøya
Olgastretet
Barentsøya
Storfjorden

Aleksandry
Ostrov Northbruk
Ostrov Gukera
Ostrov Sal'm
Ostrov Vise
Ostrov Pioner
Ostrov Oktyabr'skoy Revolyutsii

Longyearbyen
Zemlya Frantsa-Iosifa
(Franz Joseph Land)
Ostrov Uyedineniya
Ostrov Severnyy
Arktichesogo Instituta
Arkipelag Nordenshel'da

Sørkapp
Bjørnøya Bank
Svalbard
(Norway)
Bjørnøya
(Bear I.)
Hopen

Mys Karlsena
Mys Zhelaniya

Barents
Sea

Novaya Zemlya

Kara Sea

Poluo

Vesterålen
Lofoten
Nordkapp
Søroya

Murmansk

Mys Spidvel'
Mys Sukhoy Nos
Stolbovoy
Mys Chum

Ostrov Belyy
Ostrov Sverdrup
Ostrov Arktichesogo

Ostrov Vaygach
Mys Uengan
Poluostrov Yamal
Gydanskiy Poluostrov

NORWAY
OSLO
SWEDEN
STOCKHOLM

FINLAND
HELSINKI

Inarijärvi
Ozero Topozero

Kol'skiy Poluostrov
White Sea
Ostrov Kolguyev
Mys Kanin Nos
Poluostrov Kanin

Amderma
Norli'sk

Arkhangel'sk
Pechorskoye More

Vorkuta

Ostrov Severo-Yeniseyskiy

C Si P

Storsjön
Gulf of Bothnia
Oulujärvi
Petrozavodsk
Onezhskoye Ozero

Severnaya Dvina

Ukhta

Uralskiy Khrebet (Ural Mountains)

Salekhard

Novyy Urengoy

Ob'
Nizhnevartovsk

RUSSIAN FE

KØBENHAVN
BERLIN
GERMANY

TALLINN
ESTONIA
Lake Peipus
RĪGA
LATVIA
LITHUANIA
VILNIUS
Kaliningrad
RUS. FED.
MINSK

Sankt-Peterburg
Cherepovets
Ozero Il'men
Rybinskoye Vodokhranilishche
Vologda

Yaroslavl'
MOSKVA (MOSCOW)
Vladimir

Nizhniy-Novgorod
Kazan'
Izhevsk
Perm'

Kirov
Syktyvkar

Yekaterinburg
Nizhniy Tagil
Tyumen'
Irtysh

Surgut

West Siberian Plain

Tomsk
Kansk

Kemerovo
Krasnoyarsk

WARSZAWA
POLAND
PRAHA
CZECH REPUBLIC
WIEN
BRATISLAVA
SLOVAKIA

BELARUS

Smolensk
Tula
Ryazan'
Volga
Penza

Ulyanovsk

Samara
Ufa
Chelyabinsk

Kostanay

Pavlodar

Novosibirsk
Barnaul
Abakan
Zapadnyy Sayan

Rubtsovsk

Kyzyl

Vostochnyy

KYIV (KIEV)
UKRAINE

Voronezh
Saratov

Orenburg

Aktöbe

Arkalyk

ASTANA (AKMOLA)
Karaganda

Ölgiy
Altay
Altay Mountains
Uvs Nuur

M

AUSTRIA
BUDAPEST
HUNGARY
SLOVENIA
ZAGREB
CROATIA
SAN MARINO
BOSNIA HERTZ.
SARAJEVO
S&M
BEOGRAD
ROMANIA
BUCUREȘTI
MOLDOVA
CHIȘINĂU

Rostov-na-Donu
Sea of Azov
Krasnodar
Stavropol'
Elbrus 18,510

Volgograd
Astrakhan
Ural'sk
Aral'sk

Atyrau

KAZAKHSTAN

Aktau
Ustyurt Plateau

Kyzylorda

Zhezkazgan
Balkhash
Ozero Balkhash

Almaty
Pik Pobedy 24,406
Ürümqi

ITALY
ROMA
SOFIYA
BULGARIA
SKOPJE
MAC.
GREECE
TIRANE
ALBANIA

Black Sea

Sokhumi
GEORGIA
TBILISI
Groznyy

Turkmenbashi

Aral Sea
UZBEKISTAN

Dashoguz
Urganch

Syrdarya
Shymkent
TOSHKENT
BISHKEK
Pik Pobedy
KYRGYZSTAN
Korla

Qullai Garmo 24,590

Tien Shan

Tarim Pendi

Qiemo

Qilian

Tyrrhenian Sea
Sicilia
Etna 10,902
VALLETTA
MALTA
Kriti (Crete)
ATHINA (ATHENS)

İstanbul
Edirne
Bursa
İzmir
TURKEY
ANKARA
Konya
Antalya
Isparta
Adana

Samsun
Trabzon
Bat'umi
YEREVAN
ARMENIA
AZER.
BAKI
Erzurum
Sivas
Ararat 16,946
Van
Tabriz
Ardabil
Drūmīyeh

Nebitdag
ASHGABAT
Gorgān

Damāvand 18,386
TEHRAN

Mashhad
Herāt

Mary

TURKMENISTAN

Mazār-e Sharif
Samarqand
DUSHANBE
TAJIKISTAN
Kongur Shan 25,325
Hotan

Kunlun Shan
Muztag 25,338
Golmud

Mediterranean Sea
LEFKOSIA (NICOSIA)
CYPRUS
LEBANON
BEIRUT
DIMASHQ (DAMASCUS)
SYRIA
Halab
Al Mawsil

Qom
Esfahān
IRAN
Zābol
Kermān

Qandahār
Quetta

K2 28,251
Gilgit
Hindu Kush
Srinagar
Nanga Parbat 26,660
Jalalabad
Wūjang
Nanda Devi 25,645

Qingzang Gaoyuan (Plateau of Tibet)

CH

ARĀBULUS (TRIPOLI)
Gulf of Sirt
Alexandria

JERUSALEM
ISRAEL
AMMAN
JORDAN
Suez
Sinai
Al 'Aqabah

Euphrates
BAGHDAD
IRAQ
Al Başrah
Zagros Mts
Ābādān
Shīrāz
Bandar-e Abbās

AFGHANISTAN
KĀBUL
ISLAMABAD
PAKISTAN
Faisalabad
Lahore
NEW DELHI
Multan

Gurla Mandhata 25,590
Nanda Devi 25,645

Everest 29,035
Kanchenjunga 28,169
NEPAL
KATHMANDU
Namjagbarwa Feng 25,446
BHUTAN
THIMPHU
Lhasa

LIBYA
Libyan Desert
Lake Nasser

EGYPT
Nile
Red Sea

Al Madīnah
Buraydah

KUWAIT
AL KUWAYT

AL MANĀMAH
BAHRAIN
AR RIYĀD (RIYADH)
QATAR
AD DAHA (DOHA)
ABU ZABI
U.A.E.

The Gulf
Gulf of Oman
MASQAT (MUSCAT)
Ra's al Hadd

Hyderabad
Karachi
Thar Desert
Jaipur
Agra
Kanpur

DELHI
Ahmadabad
Vādodara
Indore
Narmada
Nagpur
Surat

Jazīrat Maşīrah

BANGLA-DESH
DHAKA
Kolkata (Calcutta)
Imphal
Shillong
MYANMAR (BURMA)

Tibesti
Emi Koussi 11,204
Nubian Desert

CHAD
Lake Chad
NDJAMENA

KHARTOUM
SUDAN
Jiddah
Makkah (Mecca)

SAUDI ARABIA

ERITREA
ASMARA
Ras Dashen 15,157

SAN'A'
YEMEN
Al Mukallā

'Adan (Aden)
Gulf of Aden

Suquţrā (Yemen)

Şalālah

OMAN

Arabian Sea

Arabian Basin

Mumbai (Bombay)
Pune
Deccan
Hyderabad
Krishna
Godavari

Western Ghats
Eastern Ghats

Vishakhapatnam

Bay of Bengal

Bassein
Cape Negrais
YANGON (RANGON)

VIE

CAMEROON
YAOUNDÉ
GABON
BRAZZAVILLE
CONGO
KINSHASA
LUANDA

CENTRAL AFRICAN REP.
BANGUI

Uele
DEM. REP. OF CONGO
Congo Basin

ĀDĪS ĀBEBA
ETHIOPIA
Batu 14,131

DJIBOUTI
DJIBOUTI

Shabele

SOMALIA
MUQDISHO

Socotra
Somali Basin

Owen Fracture Zone

Carlsberg Ridge

Lakshadweep (Laccadive Is) (India)

MALDIVES
MALE
Male Atoll

Chagos Archipelago
British Indian Ocean Territory
Diego Garcia

Coimbatore
Bangalore
Madurai
Chennai (Madras)

SRI JAYEWARDENEPURA KOTTE
SRI LANKA
Jaffna

North Andaman
South Andaman
Andaman Is (India)
Andaman Sea

Nicobar Is (India)
Great Nicobar

Geor

Tan

Medan

PUT

Nias

Congo
UGANDA
KAMPALA
RWANDA
KIGALI
BURUNDI
BUJUMBURA
Lake Albert
Lake Kivu

Karisimbi 14,792
Elgon 14,177
KENYA
Kirinyaga 17,060
NAIROBI
Kilimanjaro 19,341

Lake Victoria
Lake Turkana

Congo Basin

TANZANIA
DODOMA
Lake Tanganyika

Zanzibar I.
Mafia I.

VICTORIA
Mahé

Amirante Islands

SEYCHELLES
Aldabra Islands
Farquhar Group

INDIAN

OCEAN

Coco's Basin

Mid-Indian Basin

PHYSICAL MAP OF ASIA

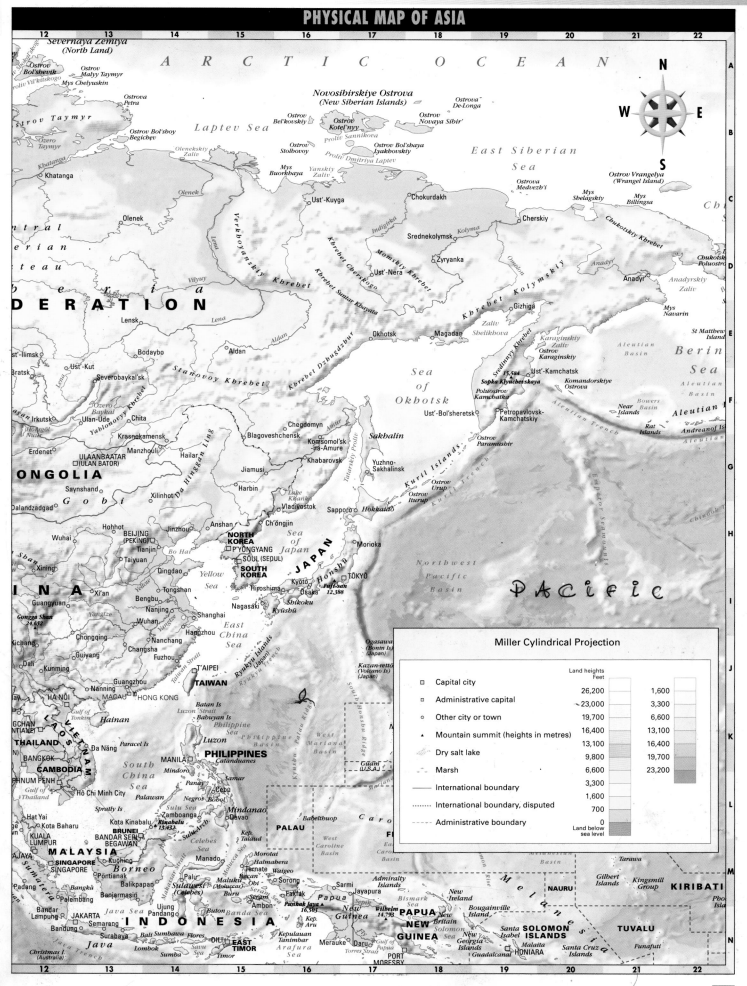

12	13	14	15	16	17	18	19	20	21	22

ARCTIC OCEAN

Severnaya Zemlya (North Land)

Ostrov Bol'shevik
Ostrov Malyy Taymyr
Mys Chelyuskin
Proliv Vil'kitskogo

Novosibirskiye Ostrova (New Siberian Islands)

Ostrova De-Longa

Ostrov Petra

Ostrov Bel'kovskiy
Ostrov Kotel'nyy
Proliv Sannikova
Ostrov Novaya Sibir'

Laptev Sea

Ostrov Taymyr
Ozero Taymyr

Ostrov Stolbovoy
Mys Buorkhaya
Yanskiy Zaliv
Proliv Dmitriya Lapteva

Ostrov Bol'shaya Lyakhovskiy

East Siberian Sea

Ostrov Vrangelya (Wrangel Island)

Khatanga

Ostrov Bol'shoy Begichev
Olenekskiy Zaliv

Chokurdakh

Mys Shelagskiy
Mys Billingsa

Ch...

Olenek

Ust'-Kuyga

Indigirka
Srednekolymsk
Kolyma

Cherskiy

Chukotskiy Khrebet

Chukotskie Poluostro

Central ... erian Plateau

Olenek

Khrebet Cherskogo
Momskiy Khrebet
Ust'-Nera
Zyryanka

Omolon

Anadyr

Anadyrskiy Zaliv

DERATION

Lensk

Lena
Vilyuy
Verkhoyanskiy Khrebet

Khrebet Suntar Khayata

Gizhiga
Khrebet Kolymskiy

Zaliv Shelikhova

Mys Navarin

Ust'-Ilimsk

Bodaybo

Aldan

Okhotsk
Magadan

St Matthew Island

Bratsk
Ust'-Kut

Severobaykal'sk

Aldan

Stanovoy Khrebet

Khrebet Dzhugdzhur

Karaginskiy Zaliv
Ostrov Karaginskiy

Berin... Sea

Aleutian Basin

Irkutsk
Ozero Baykal

Ulan-Ude

Chita

Krasnokamensk

Chegdomyn

Amur

Sea of Okhotsk

15,584
Sopka Klyuchevskaya
Poluostrov Kamchatka

Ust'-Kamchatsk

Komandorskiye Ostrova

Near Islands

Bowers Basin

Aleutian Basin

Erdenet
Manzhouli
Hailar

Blagoveshchensk

Komsomol'sk-na-Amure

Sakhalin

Petropavlovsk-Kamchatskiy

Rat Islands

Andreanof Is

Aleutian T...

ONGOLIA

ULAANBAATAR (ULAN BATOR)
Saynshand

Khabarovsk

Tatarskiy Proliv

Yuzhno-Sakhalinsk

Ust'-Bol'sheretsk

Ostrov Paramushir

Aleutian ...

Dalandzadgad

Gobi

Jiamusi

Kuril Islands

Ostrov Urup

Kuril Trench

Emperor Seamounts

Hohhot
Xilinhot
Da Hinggan Ling

Harbin

Vladivostok

Ostrov Iturup

Chinook...

Wuhai

BEIJING (PEKING)
Tianjin

Anshan

Ch'ŏngjin

Lake Khanka

Sapporo
Hokkaidō

Northwest Pacific Basin

Xining

NORTH KOREA
P'YONGYANG
SŎUL (SEOUL)
SOUTH KOREA

Sea of Japan

Morioka

Taiyuan

Bo Hai

JAPAN

Qingdao

Yellow Sea

Kyōto
Ōsaka

Honshū

TŌKYŌ
Fuji-san
12,388

PACIFIC

Xi'an
Bengbu

Tongshan

Hiroshima

Nagasaki
Kyūshū

Shikoku

INA

Guangyuan
Nanjing

Shanghai

Gongga Shan
24,652

Wuhan

Yangtze

Hangzhou

East China Sea

Kichang
Chongqing

Nanchang

Changsha

Fuzhou

Ryukyu Islands

Ogasawara (Bonin Is) (Japan)

Dali
Kunming

Guiyang

T'AIPEI

TAIWAN

Taiwan Strait

Ryukyu (Japan)

Ryukyu Trench

Kazan-rettō (Volcano Is) (Japan)

HA NỘI

Nanning

Guangzhou

MACAU
HONG KONG

Batan Is

Luzon Strait

Babuyan Is

South Honshu Ridge

Miller Cylindrical Projection

...ay
...TIANE

LAOS

Gulf of Tonkin

Hainan

Philippine Sea

Luzon

Kyushu-Palau Ridge

West Mariana Basin

THAILAND

Da Nẵng

Paracel Is

PHILIPPINES

MANILA
Catanduanes

Meridian...

Guam (U.S.A.)

BANGKOK

VIETNAM

South China Sea

Mindoro

Samar

	Land heights Feet	
□ Capital city		
□ Administrative capital	26,200	1,600
○ Other city or town	23,000	3,300
▲ Mountain summit (heights in metres)	19,700	6,600
	16,400	13,100
Dry salt lake	13,100	16,400
Marsh	9,800	19,700
International boundary	6,600	23,200
International boundary, disputed	3,300	
Administrative boundary	1,600	
	700	
	Land below sea level 0	

PHNUM PENH
CAMBODIA

Gulf of Thailand

Hồ Chí Minh City

Palawan

Panay
Cebu
Bohol
Negros

Mindanao
Davao

Babelthuop

Caro...

Hat Yai
Kota Baharu

Spratly Is

Sulu Sea

Kota Kinabalu
Zamboanga
Kinabalu
13,432
Sulu Arch.

PALAU

West Caroline Basin

Fi...

KUALA LUMPUR

BRUNEI
BANDAR SERI BEGAWAN

Celebes Sea

Morotai
Halmahera
Ternate

Manado

East Caro... Basin

...AYA

MALAYSIA

SINGAPORE
SINGAPORE

Kuching

Borneo

Pontianak

Balikpapan

Palu
Sulawesi (Celebes)

Buton

Waigeo

Obi
Buru
Seram

Melanesian Basin

Tarawa

NAURU

Gilbert Islands

Kingsmill Group

KIRIBATI

Padang

Bangka

Banjarmasin

Ujung Pandang

Makassar Strait

Bucan'

Moluccas (Maluku)

Sorong
Seram

Sarmi
Jayapura

Papua

Sepik

New Guinea

Bismarck Sea

New Ireland

Bougainville Island

Admiralty Islands

Pho... Isla...

Bandar Lampung

Palembang

JAKARTA

Semarang
Surabaya

INDONESIA

Java Sea

Bali

Java
Bandung

Lombok

Sumbawa

Flores

Savu Sea
Sumba

DILI
EAST TIMOR
Timor

Banda Sea

Kepulauan Tanimbar
Kep. Aru

Puncak Jaya
16,503

Arafura Sea

Merauke
Daru

Wilhelm
14,793

PAPUA NEW GUINEA

Gulf of Papua

PORT MORESBY

Torres Strait

Santa Isabel

SOLOMON ISLANDS

Malaita
HONIARA
Guadalcanal

New Georgia Islands

New Britain

Santa Cruz Islands

TUVALU

Funafuti

Christmas I. (Australia)

12	13	14	15	16	17	18	19	20	21	22

HABITATS

This map shows the different types of habitats across the continent.

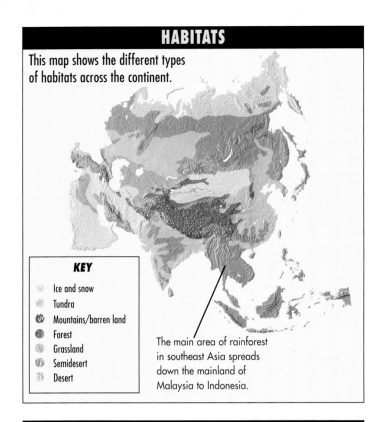

KEY

- Ice and snow
- Tundra
- Mountains/barren land
- Forest
- Grassland
- Semidesert
- Desert

The main area of rainforest in southeast Asia spreads down the mainland of Malaysia to Indonesia.

THE ASIAN RAINFOREST

In just one 10-hectare plot of Malaysian rainforest, scientists found 780 different species of trees. However, Asian rainforests are being destroyed fast.

- Around 25% of bird species and 50% of all mammal species, including the orangutan, will become extinct by 2020 if deforestation continues.

- There are only 20,000 orangutans left living in the wild. They live in Sumatra and Borneo.

- In the Tanjung Puting Park in Borneo, 6,000 orangutans live in a protected zone, along with 220 species of birds, 600 species of trees and 200 species of orchid.

• *See page 24 AMAZON RAINFOREST FACTS*
• *See page 32 HABITATS AND PROTECTING AFRICA'S RAINFOREST*

LAND USE

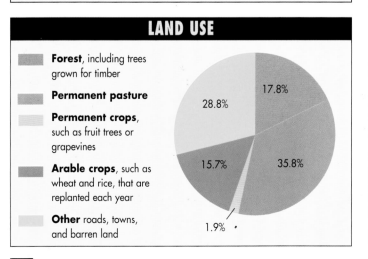

- **Forest**, including trees grown for timber
- **Permanent pasture**
- **Permanent crops**, such as fruit trees or grapevines
- **Arable crops**, such as wheat and rice, that are replanted each year
- **Other** roads, towns, and barren land

17.8%
28.8%
15.7%
35.8%
1.9%

CLIMATE: ASIA

TEMPERATURES IN JANUARY

ARCTIC CIRCLE

THE EQUATOR

KEY

- over 90° F
- 75° to 90° F
- 60° to 75° F
- 45° to 60° F
- 30° to 45° F
- 15° to 30° F
- 0° to 15° F
- -10° to 0° F
- below -10° F

TEMPERATURES IN JULY

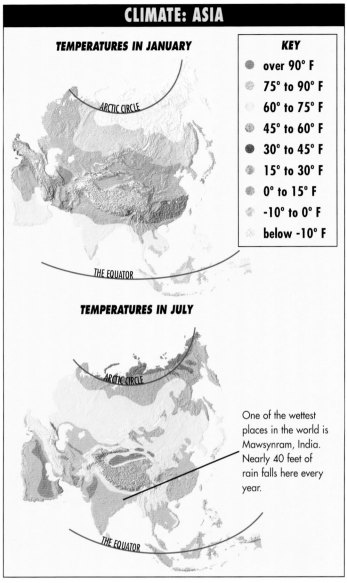

ARCTIC CIRCLE

THE EQUATOR

One of the wettest places in the world is Mawsynram, India. Nearly 40 feet of rain falls here every year.

FAST FACTS

- Indonesia is the largest archipelago, or island chain, in the world. It stretches for 3,480 miles from the Indian Ocean to the Pacific Ocean and is made up of 13,000 islands. Indonesia has about 400 volcanoes, 100 of which are active.

- The world's most spoken language is Chinese—13.69% of the world's people speak Chinese as their main language.

- The Maldives island group is made up of 1196 coral islands. Only 203 are inhabited and the average height above sea level of the islands is just 6 feet.

- The Dead Sea is a landlocked salt lake between Israel and Jordan. The Dead Sea is 1339 feet below sea level and is the lowest body of water on Earth.

- Hong Kong is made up of over 200 small islands.

Skyscrapers in Hong Kong.

ASIA FACTFILES

Each country-by-country factfile contains: **total area** of the country in square miles; **total population**; name of the **capital city**; the main **currency** used in the country; **main languages spoken** (listed in order of number of speakers); **top five farming products produced** (listed in order of importance to the country's economy); **natural resources** (of commercial importance); and a country's **status** if it is not independent.

AFGHANISTAN
Total area (sq. miles): 250,000
Total population: 29,928,987
Capital city: Kabul
Currency: Afghani (AFA)
Languages: Afghan Persian or Dari, Pashtu
Farming (top 5 products): Opium, wheat, fruit, nuts, sheep
Natural resources (top 5): Natural gas, oil, coal, copper, chromite

ARMENIA
Total area (sq. miles): 11,506
Total population: 2,982,904
Capital city: Yerevan
Currency: Dram (AMD)
Languages: Armenian, Yezidi
Farming: Fruit (especially grapes), vegetables, livestock
Natural resources (top 5): Gold, copper, molybdenum, zinc, alumina

AZERBAIJAN
Total area (sq. miles): 33,436
Total population: 7,911,974
Capital city: Baki
Currency: Azerbaijani manat (AZM)
Languages: Azerbaijani, Russian, Armenian
Farming (top 5 products): Cotton, cereal crops, rice, grapes, fruit
Natural resources: Oil, natural gas, metals (including iron)

BAHRAIN
Total area (sq. miles): 257
Total population: 453,237
Capital city: Manama
Currency: Bahraini dinar (BHD)
Languages: Arabic, English, Farsi, Urdu
Farming: Fruit, vegetables, poultry, dairy products
Natural resources: Oil, natural gas, fish, pearls

BANGLADESH
Total area (sq. miles): 55,599
Total population: 144,319,628
Capital city: Dhaka
Currency: Taka (BDT)
Languages: Bangla (or Bengali), English
Farming (top 5 products): Rice, jute, tea, wheat, sugar cane
Natural resources: Natural gas, arable land, timber, coal

BHUTAN
Total area (sq. miles): 18,147
Total population: 2,232,291
Capital city: Thimphu
Currency: Ngultrum (BTN), Indian rupee (INR)
Languages: Dzongkha, Tibetan, and Nepalese dialects
Farming (top 5 products): Rice, corn, vegetables, citrus fruits, cereal crops
Natural resources: Timber, hydroelectric power, gypsum, calcium carbonate

BRUNEI
Total area (sq. miles): 2,228
Total population: 372,361
Capital city: Bandar Seri Begawan
Currency: Bruneian dollar (BND)
Languages: Malay, English, Chinese
Farming (top 5 products): Rice, vegetables, fruit, chickens, water buffalo
Natural resources: Oil, natural gas, timber

CAMBODIA
Total area (sq. miles): 69,900
Total population: 13,607,069
Capital city: Phnom Penh
Currency: Riel (KHR)
Languages: Khmer, French, English
Farming (top 5 products): Rice, rubber, corn, vegetables, cashew nuts
Natural resources (top 5): Oil, natural gas, timber, gemstones, iron ore

CHINA
Total area (sq. miles): 3,705,407
Total population: 1,306,313,812
Capital city: Beijing
Currency: Yuan (CNY)
Languages: Mandarin Chinese
Farming (top 5 products): Rice, wheat, potatoes, corn, peanuts
Natural resources (top 5): Coal, iron ore, oil, natural gas, mercury

EAST TIMOR
Total area (sq. miles): 5,794
Total population: 1,040,880
Capital city: Dili
Currency: US dollar (USD)
Languages: Tetum, Portuguese, Indonesian, English
Farming (top 5 products): Coffee, rice, maize, cassava, sweet potatoes
Natural resources (top 5): Gold, oil, natural gas, manganese, marble

GAZA STRIP
Total area (sq. miles): 139
Total population: 1,376,289
Capital city: Gaza
Currency: New Israeli shekel (ILS)
Languages: Arabic
Farming (top 5 products): Olives, citrus fruits, vegetables, cattle, dairy products
Natural resources: Arable land, natural gas
Status: Semi-autonomous region

GEORGIA
Total area (sq. miles): 26,911
Total population: 4,677,401
Capital city: T'bilisi
Currency: Lari (GEL)
Languages: Georgian, Russian, Armenian
Farming (top 5 products): Citrus fruits, grapes, tea, hazelnuts, vegetables
Natural resources (top 5): Timber, hydroelectric power, manganese, iron ore, copper

HONG KONG
Total area (sq. miles): 422
Total population: 6,898,686
Capital city: Hong Kong
Currency: Hong Kong dollar (HKD)
Languages: Chinese, English
Farming: Vegetables, poultry
Natural resources: Deepwater harbor, feldspar
Status: Semi-autonomous territory of China

INDIA
Total area (sq. miles): 1,269,346
Total population: 1,080,264,388
Capital city: New Delhi
Currency: Indian rupee (INR)
Languages: English, Hindi, Bengali, Telugu, Marathi, Tamil, Urdu, Gujarati
Farming (top 5 products): Rice, wheat, oilseed, cotton, jute
Natural resources (top 5): Coal, iron ore, manganese, mica, bauxite

INDONESIA
Total area (sq. miles): 741,100
Total population: 241,973,879
Capital city: Jakarta
Currency: Indonesian rupiah (IDR)
Languages: Bahasa Indonesia, English, Dutch, Javanese
Farming (top 5 products): Rice, cassava, peanuts, rubber, cocoa
Natural resources (top 5): Oil, tin, natural gas, nickel, timber

IRAN
Total area (sq. miles): 636,296
Total population: 68,017,860
Capital city: Tehran
Currency: Iranian rial (IRR)
Languages: Persian, Turkic, Kurdish
Farming (top 5 products): Wheat, rice, cereal crops, sugar beets, fruit
Natural resources (top 5): Oil, natural gas, coal, chromium, copper

• See the GLOSSARY for words and terms used in these FACTFILES.

ASIA Factfiles

IRAQ

Total area (sq. miles): 168,754
Total population: 26,074,906
Capital city: Baghdad
Currency: New Iraqi dinar (NID)
Languages: Arabic, Kurdish, Assyrian, Armenian
Farming (top 5 products): Wheat, barley, rice, vegetables, dates
Natural resources (top 5): Oil, natural gas, phosphates, sulphur

ISRAEL

Total area (sq. miles): 8,019
Total population: 6,276,883
Capital city: Jerusalem
Currency: New Israeli shekel (ILS)
Languages: Hebrew, Arabic, English
Farming (top 5 products): Citrus fruits, vegetables, cotton, cattle, poultry
Natural resources (top 5): Timber, potash, copper, natural gas, phosphate

JAPAN
Total area (sq. miles): 145,883
Total population: 127,417,244
Capital city: Tokyo
Currency: Yen (JPY)
Languages: Japanese
Farming (top 5 products): Rice, sugar beets, vegetables, fruit, pigs
Natural resources: Fish

JORDAN
Total area (sq. miles): 35,637
Total population: 5,759,732
Capital city: 'Amman
Currency: Jordanian dinar (JOD)
Languages: Arabic, English
Farming (top 5 products): Wheat, barley, citrus fruits, tomatoes, melons
Natural resources: Phosphates, potash, oil shale

KAZAKHSTAN

Total area (sq. miles): 1,049,155
Total population: 15,185,844
Capital city: Astana
Currency: Tenge (KZT)
Languages: Kazakh, Russian
Farming: Cereal crops, cotton, livestock
Natural resources (top 5): Oil, natural gas, coal, iron ore, manganese

KUWAIT
Total area (sq. miles): 6,880
Total population: 1,044,294
Capital city: Kuwait
Currency: Kuwaiti dinar (KD)
Languages: Arabic, English
Farming: No farming
Natural resources: Oil, fish, shrimp, natural gas

KYRGYZSTAN

Total area (sq. miles): 76,641
Total population: 5,146,281
Capital city: Bishkek
Currency: Kyrgyz som (KGS)
Languages: Kyrgyz, Russian
Farming (top 5 products): Tobacco, cotton, potatoes, vegetables, grapes
Natural resources (top 5): Hydroelectric power, gold, coal, oil, natural gas

LAOS
Total area (sq. miles): 91,429
Total population: 6,217,141
Capital city: Vientiane
Currency: Kip (LAK)
Languages: Lao, French, English
Farming (top 5 products): Sweet potatoes, vegetables, corn, coffee, sugar cane
Natural resources (top 5): Timber, hydroelectric power, gypsum, tin, gold

LEBANON

Total area (sq. miles): 4,015
Total population: 3,826,018
Capital city: Beirut
Currency: Lebanese pound (LBP)
Languages: Arabic, French, English, Armenian
Farming (top 5 products): Citrus fruits, grapes, tomatoes, apples, vegetables
Natural resources: Limestone, iron ore, salt, surplus water (in an area where water is scarce)

MACAU
Total area (sq. miles): 9.8
Total population: 449,198
Capital city: Macau
Currency: Pataca (MOP)
Languages: Chinese (Cantonese)
Farming: Limited farming
Natural resources: Fish, shellfish
Status: Semi-autonomous territory of China

MALAYSIA
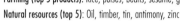
Total area (sq. miles): 127,317
Total population: 23,953,136
Capital city: Kuala Lumpur
Currency: Ringgit (MYR)
Languages: Bahasa Melayu, English, Chinese dialects, Tamil
Farming (top 5 products): Rubber, palm oil, cocoa, rice, timber
Natural resources (top 5): Tin, oil, timber, copper, iron ore

MALDIVES
Total area (sq. miles): 116
Total population: 349,106
Capital city: Male
Currency: Rufiyaa (MVR)
Languages: Maldivian Dhivehi, English spoken by government officials
Farming: Coconuts, corn, sweet potatoes
Natural resources: Fish

MONGOLIA

Total area (sq. miles): 603,909
Total population: 2,791,272
Capital city: Ulaanbaatar
Currency: Tugrik (MNT)
Languages: Khalkha Mongol, Turkic, Russian
Farming (top 5 products): Wheat, barley, vegetables, crops for animal feed, livestock (including camels and horses)
Natural resources (top 5): Oil, coal, copper, molybdenum, tungsten

MYANMAR (BURMA)

Total area (sq. miles): 261,970
Total population: 42,909,464
Capital city: Yangon (Rangoon)
Currency: Kyat (MMK)
Languages: Burmese
Farming (top 5 products): Rice, pulses, beans, sesame, groundnuts
Natural resources (top 5): Oil, timber, tin, antimony, zinc

NEPAL
Total area (sq. miles): 54,363
Total population: 27,676,547
Capital city: Kathmandu
Currency: Nepalese rupee (NPR)
Languages: Nepali, Maithali
Farming (top 5 products): Rice, corn, wheat, sugar cane, vegetables
Natural resources (top 5): Oil, natural gas, fish, salt, limestone

NORTH KOREA
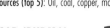
Total area (sq. miles): 46,541
Total population: 22,912,177
Capital city: Pyongyang
Currency: North Korean won (KPW)
Languages: Korean
Farming (top 5 products): Rice, corn, potatoes, soybeans, pulses
Natural resources (top 5): Coal, lead, tungsten, zinc, graphite

OMAN

Total area (sq. miles): 82,031
Total population: 2,424,290
Capital city: Muscat
Currency: Omani rial (OMR)
Languages: Arabic, English, Baluchi, Urdu, Indian dialects
Farming (top 5 products): Dates, limes, bananas, alfalfa, vegetables
Natural resources (top 5): Oil, copper, asbestos, marble, limestone

PAKISTAN
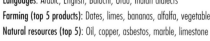
Total area (sq. miles): 310,403
Total population: 162,419,946
Capital city: Islamabad
Currency: Pakistani rupee (PKR)
Languages: Punjabi, Sindhi, Siraiki, Pashtu, Urdu
Farming (top 5 products): Cotton, wheat, rice, sugar cane, fruit
Natural resources (top 5): Natural gas, oil, coal, iron ore, copper

PHILIPPINES
Total area (sq. miles): 115,831
Total population: 87,857,473
Capital city: Manila
Currency: Philippine peso (PHP)
Languages: Filipino, English, Tagalog, Cebuano
Farming (top 5 products): Sugar cane, coconuts, rice, corn, bananas
Natural resources (top 5): Timber, oil, nickel, cobalt, silver

QATAR
Total area (sq. miles): 4416
Total population: 863,051
Capital city: Doha
Currency: Qatari rial (QAR)
Languages: Arabic, English
Farming (top 5 products): Fruit, vegetables, poultry, dairy products, cattle
Natural resources: Oil, natural gas, fish

SAUDI ARABIA
Total area (sq. miles): 756,985
Total population: 20,841,523
Capital city: Riyadh
Currency: Saudi riyal (SAR)
Languages: Arabic
Farming (top 5 products): Wheat, barley, tomatoes, melons, dates
Natural resources (top 5): Oil, natural gas, iron ore, gold, copper

SINGAPORE
Total area (sq. miles): 267
Total population: 4,425,720
Capital city: Singapore
Currency: Singapore dollar (SGD)
Languages: Chinese (Mandarin), English, Malay
Farming (top 5 products): Rubber, copra, fruit, orchids, vegetables
Natural resources: Fish, deepwater ports (suitable for shipping)

SOUTH KOREA
Total area (sq. miles): 38,023
Total population: 48,422,644
Capital city: Seoul
Currency: South Korean won (KRW)
Languages: Korean
Farming (top 5 products): Rice, vegetables, barley, vegetables, fruit
Natural resources (top 5): Coal, tungsten, graphite, molybdenum, lead

SRI LANKA
Total area (sq. miles): 25,332
Total population: 20,064,776
Capital city: Sri Jayewardenepura Kotte
Currency: Sri Lankan rupee (LKR)
Languages: Sinhala, Tamil, English
Farming (top 5 products): Rice, sugar cane, cereal crops, pulses, oilseed
Natural resources (top 5): Limestone, graphite, mineral sands, gemstones, phosphates

SYRIA
Total area (sq. miles): 71,498
Total population: 18,448,752
Capital city: Damascus
Currency: Syrian pound (SYP)
Languages: Arabic, Kurdish
Farming (top 5 products): Wheat, barley, cotton, lentils, chickpeas
Natural resources (top 5): Oil, phosphates, chrome ore, manganese, asphalt

TAIWAN
Total area (sq. miles): 13,892
Total population: 22,894,384
Capital city: Taipei
Currency: New Taiwan dollar (TWD)
Languages: Chinese (Mandarin), Taiwanese
Farming (top 5 products): Rice, corn, vegetables, fruit, tea
Natural resources (top 5): Coal, natural gas, limestone, marble, asbestos
Status: Self-governing territory of China

TAJIKISTAN
Total area (sq. miles): 55,251
Total population: 7,163,506
Capital city: Dushanbe
Currency: Somoni
Languages: Tajik, Russian
Farming (top 5 products): Cotton, cereal crops, fruit, grapes, vegetables
Natural resources (top 5): Hydroelectric power, oil, uranium, mercury, coal

THAILAND
Total area (sq. miles): 198,457
Total population: 65,444,371
Capital city: Bangkok
Currency: Baht (THB)
Languages: Thai, English
Farming (top 5 products): Rice, cassava, rubber, corn, sugar cane
Natural resources (top 5): Tin, rubber, natural gas, tungsten, tantalum

TURKMENISTAN
Total area (sq. miles): 188,456
Total population: 4,952,081
Capital city: Ashgabat
Currency: Turkmen manat (TMM)
Languages: Turkmen, Russian, Uzbek
Farming: Cotton, cereal crops, livestock
Natural resources: Oil, natural gas, sulphur, salt

UNITED ARAB EMIRATES
Total area (sq. miles): 32,000
Total population: 957,133
Capital city: Abu Dhabi
Currency: Emirati dirham (AED)
Languages: Arabic, Persian, English, Hindi, Urdu
Farming (top 5 products): Dates, vegetables, water melons, poultry, eggs
Natural resources: Oil, natural gas

UZBEKISTAN
Total area (sq. miles): 172,742
Total population: 26,851,195
Capital city: Toshkent
Currency: Uzbekistani sum (UZS)
Languages: Uzbek, Russian, Tajik
Farming (top 5 products): Cotton, vegetables, fruit, cereal crops, livestock
Natural resources (top 5): Natural gas, oil, coal, gold, uranium

VIETNAM
Total area (sq. miles): 127,244
Total population: 83,535,576
Capital city: Hanoi
Currency: Dong (VND)
Languages: Vietnamese, English, French, Chinese, Khmer
Farming (top 5 products): Rice, coffee, rubber, cotton, tea
Natural resources (top 5): Phosphates, coal, manganese, bauxite, chromate

WEST BANK
Total area (sq. miles): 2,263
Total population: 2,385,615
Capital city: West Bank
Currency: New Israeli shekel (ILS), Jordanian dinar (JOD)
Languages: Arabic, Hebrew, English
Farming (top 5 products): Olives, citrus fruits, vegetables, cattle, dairy products
Natural resources: Arable land
Status: Disputed territory

YEMEN
Total area (sq. miles): 203,850
Total population: 20,727,063
Capital city: Sanaa
Currency: Yemeni rial (YER)
Languages: Arabic
Farming (top 5 products): Cereal crops, fruit, vegetables, pulses, qat (a mildly narcotic shrub)
Natural resources (top 5): Oil, fish, rock salt, marble, coal

• See the GLOSSARY for words and terms used in these FACTFILES.

Tigers are the largest member of the cat family. They live in a variety of habitats in southeast Asia—from hot jungle regions in countries such as India, to the cold, coniferous forests of Siberia.

• See page 55
OCEANIA FACTFILES

The term *Oceania* generally refers to the countries of Australia, New Zealand, Papua New Guinea, and the islands of the South Pacific. Oceania stretches across a vast area of ocean and includes 20,000 or so islands that make up the regions of Micronesia, Melanesia and Polynesia. Thousands of the islands are uninhabited, and many are formed from coral reefs and underwater volcanoes. Papua New Guinea is made up of the eastern half of the island of New Guinea and around 600 smaller islands.

The Great Barrier Reef is a complex of coral reefs, sandbanks, and islets off the northeastern coast of Australia.

FAST FACTS

- The Great Barrier Reef spreads for 1,250 miles along Australia's coast. It covers an area of 135,000 square miles.

- The capital of New Zealand, Wellington, is the southernmost capital city in the world.

- Australia has a total of 529,346 square miles of desert—18% of Australia is desert land.

- The Kwajalein atoll, in the Marshall Islands, is a ring of coral enclosing a lagoon of around 1,100 square miles. It is the biggest atoll in the world.

- The Marshall islands comprise two island chains which include 30 atolls and 1,152 islands.

- The 5.5 million people of Papua New Guinea speak around 800 different languages.

- New Zealand uses hydro-electric power and has very little industry so it is one of the cleanest, least-polluted countries in the world.

HIGHEST MOUNTAINS (BY COUNTRY)

NAME	LOCATION	HEIGHT (feet)
Mt Wilhelm	Papua New Guinea	14,793
Mt Cook	New Zealand	12,316
Mt Kosciuszko	Australia	7,316

LARGEST ISLANDS

NAME	LOCATION	AREA (sq. miles)
New Guinea Island (total island including Indonesian part)		316,990
South Island	New Zealand	58,108
North Island	New Zealand	44,286
Tasmania	Australia	26,178

* Australia is too large to be an island. It is a continental landmass.

HABITATS

This map shows the different types of habitat across the continent.

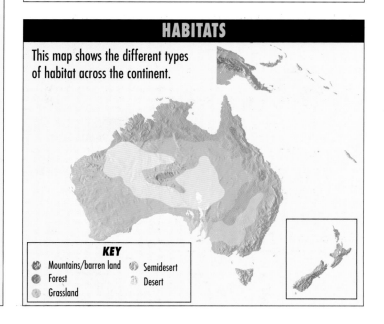

KEY

- Mountains/barren land
- Forest
- Grassland
- Semidesert
- Desert

POLITICAL MAP OF OCEANIA

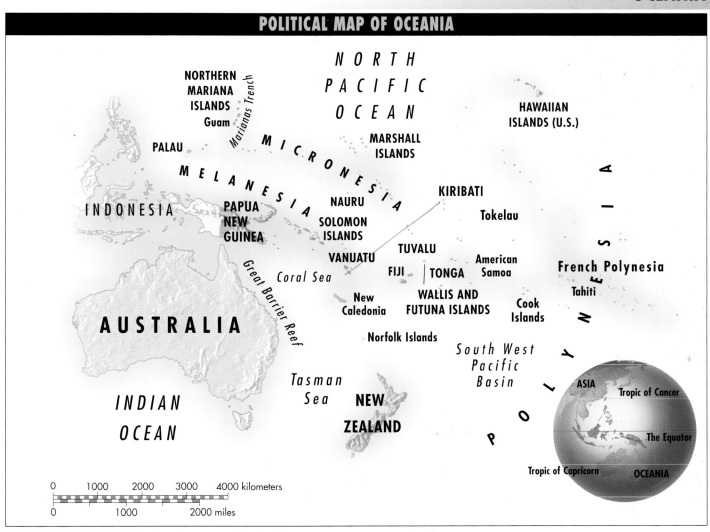

NORTH
PACIFIC
OCEAN

NORTHERN
MARIANA
ISLANDS
Guam

Marianas Trench

HAWAIIAN
ISLANDS (U.S.)

M I C R O N E S I A

PALAU

MARSHALL
ISLANDS

M E L A N E S I A

INDONESIA

PAPUA
NEW
GUINEA

NAURU

KIRIBATI

Tokelau

SOLOMON
ISLANDS

TUVALU

VANUATU

FIJI

TONGA

American
Samoa

French Polynesia

Tahiti

Coral Sea

New
Caledonia

WALLIS AND
FUTUNA ISLANDS

Cook
Islands

P O L Y N E S I A

AUSTRALIA

Great Barrier Reef

Norfolk Islands

South West
Pacific
Basin

Tasman
Sea

NEW
ZEALAND

INDIAN
OCEAN

ASIA

Tropic of Cancer

The Equator

Tropic of Capricorn

OCEANIA

0   1000   2000   3000   4000 kilometers

0   1000   2000 miles

ULURU

Uluru in the desert of central Australia is a sacred place to Australian aboriginal people. This oval-shaped, giant block of sandstone is at least 450 million years old. Uluru is 2.2 miles long and 1.5 miles wide.

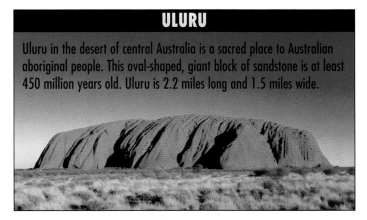

LAND USE

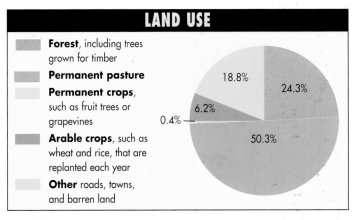

- **Forest**, including trees grown for timber
- **Permanent pasture**
- **Permanent crops**, such as fruit trees or grapevines
- **Arable crops**, such as wheat and rice, that are replanted each year
- **Other** roads, towns, and barren land

18.8%
24.3%
6.2%
0.4%
50.3%

CLIMATE: OCEANIA

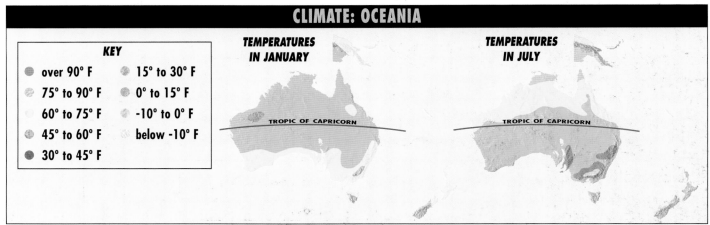

KEY

- over 90° F
- 75° to 90° F
- 60° to 75° F
- 45° to 60° F
- 30° to 45° F
- 15° to 30° F
- 0° to 15° F
- -10° to 0° F
- below -10° F

TEMPERATURES IN JANUARY

TROPIC OF CAPRICORN

TEMPERATURES IN JULY

TROPIC OF CAPRICORN

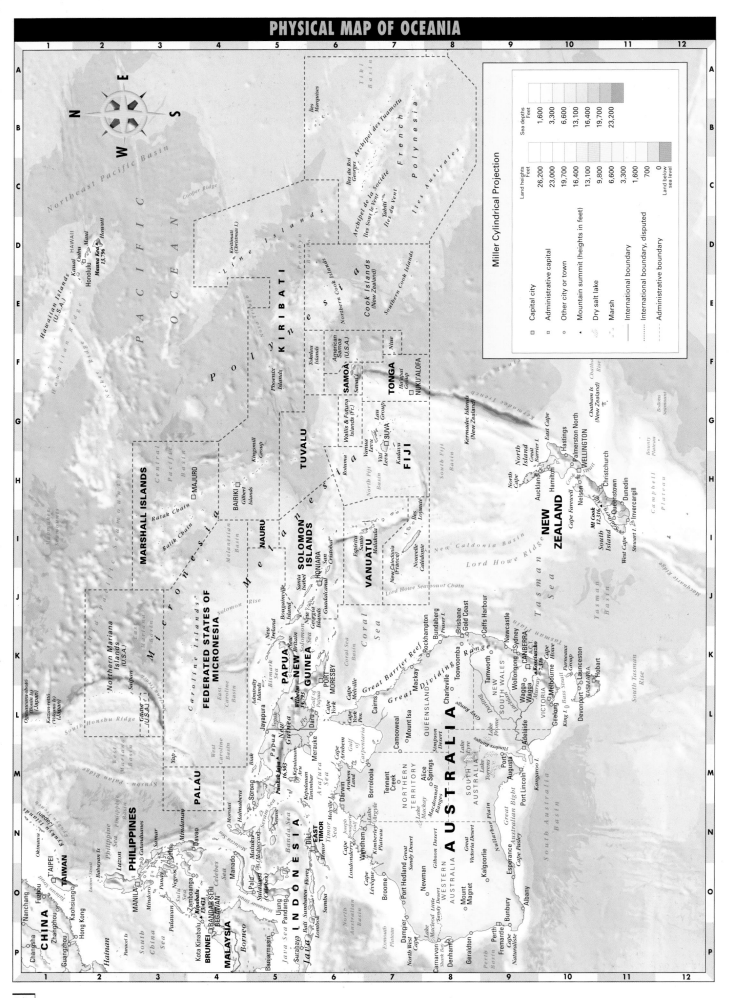

OCEANIA FACTFILES

Each country-by-country factfile contains: **total area** of the country in square miles; **total population**; name of the **capital city**; the main **currency** used in the country; **main languages spoken** (listed in order of number of speakers); **top five farming products produced** (listed in order of importance to the country's economy); **natural resources** (of commercial importance); and a country's **status** if it is not independent.

AMERICAN SAMOA

Total area (sq. miles): 77
Total population: 57,881
Capital city: Pago Pago
Currency: US dollar (USD)
Languages: Samoan, English
Farming: Bananas, coconuts, vegetables, taro
Natural resources: Pumice
Status: United States unincorporated territory

AUSTRALIA
Total area (sq. miles): 2,967,909
Total population: 20,090,437
Capital city: Canberra
Currency: Australian dollar (AUD)
Languages: English
Farming (top 5 products): Wheat, barley, sugar cane, fruit, livestock
Natural resources (top 5): Bauxite, coal, iron ore, copper, tin

COOK ISLANDS
Total area (sq. miles): 93
Total population: 21,388
Capital city: Avarua
Currency: New Zealand dollar (NZD)
Languages: English, Maori
Farming (top 5 products): Copra, citrus fruits, pineapples, tomatoes, beans
Natural resources: No natural resources
Status: New Zealand overseas territory

FIJI
Total area (sq. miles): 7,054
Total population: 893,354
Capital city: Suva
Currency: Fijian dollar (FJD)
Languages: English, Fijian, Hindustani
Farming (top 5 products): Sugar cane, coconuts, cassava, rice, sweet potatoes
Natural resources (top 5): Timber, fish, gold, copper, oil potential

FRENCH POLYNESIA
Total area (sq. miles): 1,609
Total population: 270,485
Capital city: Papeete
Currency: Comptoirs Francais du Pacifique franc (XPF)
Languages: French, Polynesian
Farming (top 5 products): Coconuts, vanilla, vegetables, fruit, poultry
Natural resources: Timber, fish, cobalt, hydroelectric power
Status: French overseas territory

GUAM
Total area (sq. miles): 212
Total population: 168,564
Capital city: Hagatna
Currency: US dollar (USD)
Languages: English, Chamorro, Philippine languages
Farming (top 5 products): Fruit, copra, vegetables, eggs, livestock
Natural resources: Fish
Status: United States unincorporated territory

KIRIBATI
Total area (sq. miles): 313
Total population: 103,092
Capital city: Tarawa
Currency: Australian dollar (AUD)
Languages: I-Kiribati, English
Farming: Copra, taro, breadfruit, vegetables
Natural resources: No natural resources

MARSHALL ISLANDS

Total area (sq. miles): 70
Total population: 59,071
Capital city: Majuro
Currency: US dollar (USD)
Languages: Marshallese, English
Farming (top 5 products): Coconuts, tomatoes, melons, taro, breadfruit
Natural resources: Coconuts, fish, deep seabed minerals

MICRONESIA (FEDERATED STATES OF)

Total area (sq. miles): 271
Total population: 108,105
Capital city: Palikir
Currency: US dollar (USD)
Languages: English, Trukese, Pohnpeian, Yapese, Kosrean, Ulithian
Farming (top 5 products): Black pepper, tropical fruit and vegetables, coconuts, cassava, betel nuts
Natural resources: Timber, fish, deep seabed minerals, phosphate

NAURU

Total area (sq. miles): 8
Total population: 13,048
Capital city: No capital – government offices in Yaren district
Currency: Australian dollar (AUD)
Languages: Nauruan, English
Farming: Coconuts
Natural resources: Phosphates, fish

NEW CALEDONIA

Total area (sq. miles): 7,359
Total population: 216,494
Capital city: Noumea
Currency: Comptoirs Francais du Pacifique franc (XPF)
Languages: French, 33 Melanesian-Polynesian dialects
Farming: Vegetables, livestock (including deer)
Natural resources (top 5): Nickel, chrome, iron, cobalt, manganese
Status: French overseas territory

NEW ZEALAND

Total area (sq. miles): 103,738
Total population: 4,035,461
Capital city: Wellington
Currency: New Zealand dollar (NZD)
Languages: English, Maori
Farming (top 5 products): Wheat, barley, potatoes, pulses, fruit
Natural resources (top 5): Natural gas, iron ore, sand, coal, timber

NORTHERN MARIANA ISLANDS

Total area (sq. miles): 184
Total population: 80,362
Capital city: Saipan
Currency: US dollar (USD)
Languages: Philippine languages, Chinese, Chamorro, English
Farming: Coconuts, fruit, vegetables, cattle
Natural resources: Arable land, fish
Status: United States commonwealth

PALAU

Total area (sq. miles): 177
Total population: 20,303
Capital city: Koror
Currency: US dollar (USD)
Languages: Palauan, English, Tobi, Angaur
Farming: Coconuts, copra, cassava, sweet potatoes
Natural resources: Timber, gold, fish, deep seabed minerals

PAPUA NEW GUINEA

Total area (sq. miles): 178,704
Total population: 5,545,268
Capital city: Port Moresby
Currency: Kina (PGK)
Languages: Melanesian, up to 800 indigenous languages
Farming (top 5 products): Coffee, cocoa, coconuts, palm kernels, tea
Natural resources (top 5): Gold, copper, silver, natural gas, timber

SAMOA

Total area (sq. miles): 1,137
Total population: 177,287
Capital city: Apia
Currency: Tala (SAT)
Languages: Samoan, English
Farming (top 5 products): Coconuts, bananas, taro, yams, coffee
Natural resources: Timber, fish, hydroelectric power

SOLOMON ISLANDS

Total area (sq. miles): 10,985
Total population: 538,032
Capital city: Honiara
Currency: Solomon Islands dollar (SBD)
Languages: Melanesian, English, 120 indigenous languages
Farming (top 5 products): Cocoa, coconuts, palm kernels, rice, potatoes
Natural resources (top 5): Fish, timber, gold, bauxite, phosphates

TONGA

Total area (sq. miles): 289
Total population: 112,422
Capital city: Nuku'alofa
Currency: Pa'anga (TOP)
Languages: Tongan, English
Farming (top 5 products): Squash, coconuts, copra, bananas, vanilla
Natural resources: Fish

TUVALU

Total area (sq. miles): 10
Total population: 11,636
Capital city: Funafuti
Currency: Australian dollar (AUD)
Languages: Tuvaluan, English, Samoan, Kiribati (on island of Nui)
Farming: Coconuts
Natural resources: Fish

VANUATU

Total area (sq. miles): 4,710
Total population: 205,754
Capital city: Port-Vila
Currency: Vatu (VUV)
Languages: English, French, 100 indigenous languages
Farming (top 5 products): Copra, coconuts, cocoa, coffee, taro
Natural resources: Manganese, timber, fish

WALLIS AND FUTUNA ISLANDS

Total area (sq. miles): 106
Total population: 16,025
Capital city: Mata-Utu
Currency: Comptoirs Francais du Pacifique franc (XPF)
Languages: Wallisian, Futunian, French
Farming (top 5 products): Breadfruit, yams, taro, bananas, livestock
Natural resources: No natural resources
Status: French overseas territory

• See the GLOSSARY for words and terms used in these FACTFILES.

Size of Arctic Ocean:
5.4 million square miles

The Ice Cap:
The Arctic Ocean is surrounded by icy land. A large section of the ocean is permanently frozen. This is called the *ice cap*. In the winter, the sea freezes and increases the size of the ice cap so that it touches the land.

Arctic temperatures:
Lowest winter temperature -49°F

Arctic seasons:
The sun never rises during the six months of the Arctic winter. In the summer, there are times when the sun never sets.

Arctic animal life:
Polar bears, caribou, arctic foxes, seals, whales, narwhals, walruses, and sea birds all live in the Arctic.

Polar bear fact:
The polar bear is the only bear with international protection. Scientists estimate there are up to 40,000 polar bears living in the Arctic Circle.

Polar bear hunting grounds:
Polar bears spend the winter and spring on the frozen ocean hunting for harp seals and hooded seals. When the ice thaws for the summer, they move back onto the mainland.

Plant life:
Over 500 different species of flowering plants grow within the Arctic Circle.

Fast fact:
Both the Arctic and Antarctic are classified as *cold deserts* because most areas receive less than 10 inches of rain or snow each year.

THE ARCTIC

The Arctic region is at the very top of the Earth. The Arctic Circle comprises a shallow, frozen ocean surrounded by the northern edges of Europe, Asia, and North America. The area is named after *Arktos*, the Great Bear star constellation, which dominates the northern polar skies. The Arctic circle area is marked on maps with an imaginary line.

Polar bears live in the Arctic Circle. They are the world's largest land-living predator.

POLITICAL MAP OF THE ARCTIC

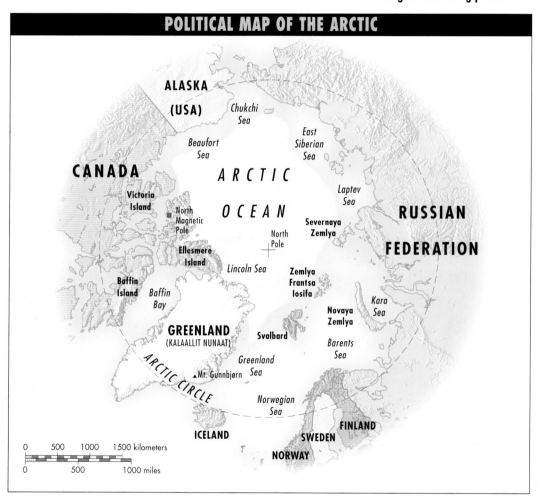

THE ARCTIC ICE

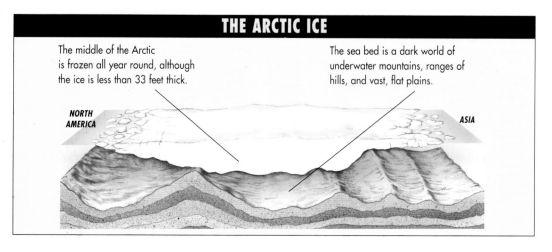

The middle of the Arctic is frozen all year round, although the ice is less than 33 feet thick.

The sea bed is a dark world of underwater mountains, ranges of hills, and vast, flat plains.

ANTARCTICA

Antarctica is a mountainous continent that is almost completely covered by a gigantic sheet of ice the size of Europe and the USA put together. It is the coldest and windiest place on Earth. Average winter temperatures reach -76°F and roaring, ferocious winds of up to 180 miles an hour produce blizzards and snowdrifts.

Emperor Penguins live in the Antarctic. They grow to around 3.5 feet tall and are the largest species of penguin.

ANTARCTICA FACTFILE

SOUTH AMERICA

ANTARCTICA

Antarctic Circle

Antarctica/Arctic:
The name means *opposite the Arctic*. When it is summer in the Arctic, it is winter in Antarctica.

Total area of continent:
5,443,000 square miles
98% ice
2% barren rock

Life in Antarctica:
The Antarctic has very little ice-free land even in summer. No land mammals live here. Fewer plants and animals live here than the Arctic. Adelie and Emperor penguins come ashore to breed and lay their eggs here.

Nearest landmass:
South America—the southern tip is approximately 600 miles from Antarctica.

Length of coastline:
11,164,798 miles

Highest mountain:
Vinson Massif
16,066 feet

Lowest point:
Bentley sub-glacial trench
8,383 feet below sea level

Population:
No permanent population. Around 1,000 to 4,000 scientists working at research stations.

Natural resources:
Iron ore, chromium, copper, gold, nickel, platinum, and other minerals.

Fast fact:
More than 90% of all the world's fresh water is stored in the ice sheets on Antarctica, and Greenland in the Arctic region.

POLITICAL MAP OF ANTARCTICA

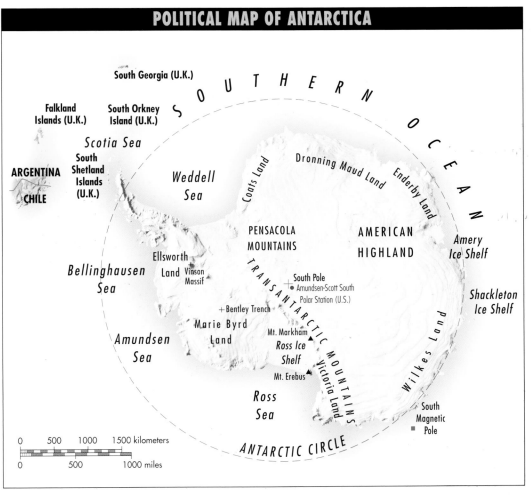

South Georgia (U.K.)

SOUTHERN OCEAN

Falkland Islands (U.K.)

South Orkney Island (U.K.)

Scotia Sea

South Shetland Islands (U.K.)

ARGENTINA

CHILE

Weddell Sea

Coats Land

Dronning Maud Land

Enderby Land

PENSACOLA MOUNTAINS

AMERICAN HIGHLAND

Amery Ice Shelf

Ellsworth Land

Vinson Massif

Bellinghausen Sea

TRANSANTARCTIC MOUNTAINS

South Pole
Amundsen-Scott South Polar Station (U.S.)

Shackleton Ice Shelf

+Bentley Trench

Marie Byrd Land

Mt. Markham

Ross Ice Shelf

Wilkes Land

Amundsen Sea

Mt. Erebus

Victoria Land

South Magnetic Pole

Ross Sea

ANTARCTIC CIRCLE

0 500 1000 1500 kilometers
0 500 1000 miles

THE ANTARCTIC ICE

The Antarctic ice sheet is up to 2.5 miles thick in places.

A few mountains, called *nunataks*, extend their peaks above the ice.

If the ice was removed, the land would rise about 1800 feet.

WEST

EAST

GLOSSARY

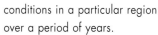

Afrikaans A language of South Africa, closely related to Dutch.

Amerindian A word used to describe Native Americans, or American Indians. When Christopher Columbus reached the Americas, he thought he had reached Asia and the East Indies, which is why the word Indian first came to be used in connection with people living in America.

Arable land Land that is suitable for growing crops.

Aragonite A mineral consisting of calcium carbonate. It can be found in white sea shells and as deposits in hot springs (naturally hot water heated by underground volcanic activity).

Archipelago A group of islands, or an area of sea containing many islands.

Atoll A ring-shaped reef, island, or chain of islands formed from coral.

Bantu A "language family" used by over 400 different ethnic groups in Africa from Cameroon to South Africa.

Bauxite The ore from which aluminium is extracted.

Berber People belonging to northwest Africa, chiefly living in Morocco and Algeria, although some now live in Egypt and as far south as Burkina Faso.

Borders Lines separating geographical or political areas, especially the edges of countries. Borders are normally drawn up by governments. Borders can change over time as countries take over new territory, join with other countries, or split into smaller countries.

Calcium carbonate An insoluble, white solid which can be found in marble, chalk, limestone, and calcite, and in sea shells and some corals. It is used to make cement.

Cassava The starchy, tuber-like root of a tropical tree. It is used as food, and is sometimes called *manioc*.

Chain (of mountains) A line of mountains made up of more than one mountain range.

Chicle A milky, latex liquid obtained from the sapodilla tree. It is used to make chewing gum.

Climate The average temperature and weather conditions in a particular region over a period of years.

Continent One of the Earth's large, continuous landmasses: Africa, Antarctica, Asia, Australia, Europe, North America, and South America.

Copra The oil-yielding kernel of the coconut.

Coral The hard, stony substance secreted by marine animals called *polyps* as an external skeleton.

Coral reef An underwater structure made from coral—the hard, external skeletons of marine animals called *polyps*. When a polyp dies, its skeleton remains as part of the reef so the reef gradually becomes larger.

Creole A language formed from the mixing of a local language and a European language, such as French.

Desert A barren area of land with very little or no rainfall. Deserts are normally sandy or rocky with limited plant and animal life. Deserts can be hot or cold.

Equator An imaginary line around the center of the Earth. The equator is exactly halfway between the North and South Poles, the most northern and southern points on the Earth, and the axis points the Earth spins on. The Equator divides the Earth into the northern and southern hemispheres.

Faults Cracks in the Earth's crust. The movement of the Earth's tectonic plates causes rocks to move and stretch until the pressure becomes so great that they crack.

Geothermal power Power created for use in homes or industry using the Earth's internal heat. In Iceland, the steam from seawater boiled by molten lava, 1.2 miles below the ground, is used by power stations to heat fresh water for homes, and to power turbines to produce electricity.

Gorge A valley with steep, rocky sides between hills or mountains. Gorges are formed over a long time by a river cutting down into the land it flows across.

Graphite A gray form of carbon which occurs in some rocks. Graphite has many uses, including the writing part of pencils.

Hydroelectric power The generation of electricity for use in homes and industry using flowing water. The water is used to drive turbines to power generators.

indigenous Originating or occurring naturally within a country or a region. It can refer to people, plants, or animals.

Infant mortality rate The number of deaths of infants under one year old in a year. It is a measure of the quality of life in a country, including health and wealth.

Kaolin A fine, soft white clay used in the production of china and porcelain and in some medicines.

Lava Hot, molten rock expelled from a volcano. When the lava is still inside the Earth it is called magma.

Life expectancy The average number of years a person can be expected to live in a given place. It is a measure of the quality of life in a country, including health and wealth.

Lignite A type of soft, brown coal.

Longitude Lines on a map which run north to south and measure how many degrees east or west a place is from the *Prime Meridian Line* (the imaginary line that runs north to south through Greenwich in London, UK, the place that has been designated zero degrees longitude).

Magma Hot, molten rock inside the Earth's mantle. Magma sometimes escapes to the Earth's surface through a volcano or other crack in the Earth's crust. As soon as it leaves the Earth, magma is called *lava*.

Manganese A metallic element, mined and used in the making of steel, pesticides, fertilizers, batteries, and some ceramics. It is a hazardous substance. High levels of manganese will hurt the nervous system.

Mantle The layer inside the Earth between the Earth's rocky crust and the core. The mantle is made up of soft, molten rock.

Mayan A "language family" that includes many American Indian languages spoken by people in Central America.

Molybdenum A brittle, silver-gray metal used in making some kinds of steel.

Nahua A language spoken by indigenous people from southern Mexico to Central America. The language dates back to the Aztecs.

Oil shale Fine-grained, sedimentary rock from which oil can be extracted. Sedimentary rock is formed from particles of mud, sand, and other debris that have settled and been squashed down to form hard rock.

Ore Rock that contains a metal that can be extracted.

Papiamento A Spanish Creole language which is mixed with Portuguese, Dutch, and some English. It is spoken on some Caribbean islands.

Patois A simplified spoken form of a language, often French or English, that has been adapted by people in a particular region.

Population The total number of people living in a town, city, particular area, country, or continent.

Pyrethrum A member of the chrysanthemum family that is used to make pesticides.

Quechua A language spoken by around 13 million people in South America. Quechua was spoken by the Incas.

Rainforest A tropical forest made up of four layers:

The emergent layer: Giant trees that grow above the canopy as high as 240 feet.

The canopy: Most of the rainforest wildlife is found in the canopy, 130 feet above the ground. This layer receives the most rain and sunshine so leaves, flowers, and fruit grow here.

The understory: A layer of smaller trees, climbing plants and shrubs that are able to live in the shade.

The forest floor: The ground is almost bare except for a thin layer of leaves. Very little sunlight filters down to here.

The rainforests act as a global air conditioner by absorbing carbon dioxide from the air, storing the carbon, and releasing fresh, clean oxygen. The world loses 50 species of plants and animals every day due to rainforest deforestation—many before they have been cataloged and studied.

Range (of mountains) A group of mountains.

Sea level The level of the sea's surface. It is used as the starting point for measuring the height of the surrounding land and landforms such as hills and mountains.

Seismic waves The vibrations caused by an earthquake, the underground movement of rocks. Some waves travel at over 13,000 mph, but can only be felt when they reach the surface.

Sisal A plant that produces a fiber suitable for making ropes and matting.

Sorghum A cereal crop widely grown in Africa. It can be used as a grain for food and as animal feed.

Taiga The vast stretch of coniferous forest that reaches across northern Asia close to the Arctic Circle.

Taro A tropical plant with edible leaves and edible, starchy corms.

Tectonic plates The huge pieces of the Earth's crust fit together like a puzzle. There are oceanic plates and continental plates. The plates are constantly moving, by just a few inches each year, sliding and pushing against each other.

Tides The rise and then fall of the water in the world's oceans that happens twice each day. Tides are caused by the pull of the Moon's gravity. As the Earth spins and parts of its surface move past the moon, the water rises as the Moon pulls it—this is called a *high tide*. At the same time, parts of the Earth's surface that are not facing the Moon have a low tide.

Tropic of Cancer An imaginary line that runs around the world between the North Pole and the Equator. These lines are used to measure the Earth and to help find places and describe different regions. The area between the Tropic of Cancer and the Tropic of Capricorn is warm and wet and is known as the *Tropics*.

Tropic of Capricorn An imaginary line that runs around the world between the South Pole and the Equator. The area between the Tropic of Capricorn and the Tropic of Cancer is warm and wet and is known as the *Tropics*.

Tundra A boggy landscape of low-growing plants and lakes that form over permafrost—a layer of permanently frozen soil found beneath the surface of many cold areas.

INDEX

The letters a, b, c, d following the page number indicate the column (from left to right) where the information may be found on that page.